I0429100

When You're Food: Raw

A Fighter's View of Predatory Aggression:
The Forever Autumn Press Edition

Dust Cover

A Forever Autumn Press Book

In **When You're Food**, James LaFond elevates the art of extreme political incorrectness to its uncomfortable apogee in this very personal exploration of human-on-human predation in Baltimore Maryland.

Engaging urban survival guide, brutal oral history and outrageous memoir, this disturbing book makes the case that civilization is a lie, human society is essentially cannibalistic, and **you** are on the menu.

"James' first book spoke to me as an angry confused young man. He was not an ass-kicking machine, took public transportation and was the only author in the field to address the racial nuances of urban violence. **When You're Food** is his masterpiece..."
        -Dominick Mattero

"**When You're Food** is a gripping examination of the roiling violence that thrives behind the mask of societal convention and the veneer of law and order..."
        -Professor David Carl

When You're Food

For more information on the author and his
ongoing update of the Harm City hunting matrix, go
to www.jameslafond.com

Cover: Saturn Devouring His Son by Francisco Goya

The Forever Autumn Press Library

When You're Food: Raw 2015
The Boned Zone 2015
An Arabian Terror Tale 2015
Hemavore 2015
VielsDen Keep Vol 1 2015

To Assemble the Dead 2016
Autumn in Babylon 2016
Junger Hass: Collected Poems, Art and Plays 2016
Asylum Girls Club #1 2016
VielsDen Keep Vol 2 2016
L'asile Des Vampires Vol 1 2016

When You're Food

Contents

When You're Food

When You're Food: Raw

Introduction to the Forever Autumn Press Edition

This book you are holding in your hand is one of the best horror novellas you will ever read. There are no vampires in it although it can be argued that we live in a vampire state, a Nosferatu nation. There are no werewolves in it, although the hero is a bit hairy on his face and he works when the moon is out. Zombies? Well there are the living brain dead whose numbers increase exponentially every day in the former british trading post abortion called Murica. The only spirits within this book is the Spirit of Age itself; the rotting zeitgeist of a dying country. Like Countess Bathory keeping herself young (or so she thought) with the blood of murdered virgins, they are going to keep this mess going for as long as possible. There is no way they can wield power with an actual solution, instead they keep an endless hobbesian state of war going to feed the furnace of the machine. Like the moloch scene in Metropolis. The Aztec God Emperors had nothing on our modern day overlords. Life is a horror film that never stops and the villains have won...

James LaFond is your crypt keeper here, punctuating his narration with black humor and a self effacement that is a mark of wisdom. Of course he would never admit this, further solidifying his modest reputation, but I digress. I first read this book as a word processor generated collection in an old 99 cent back to school sale binder, then as a printed PDF e-book bound with clip binders. Finally, thanks to the leviathan online retail outfit named after the mythical and metaphorical female warriors of the ancient world, a legit printed version has since become available with a stunning vomit colored and quite imaginative cover consisting of only the title in the center of the book.

This unknown classic is still Mister Jim's best-selling book, his critical masterpiece anyhow. The book is the perfect length, with both a chilling opening and a nail biting and hilarious ending. It fulfills the concept, or at least my concept, of horror. Appealing to the primal fear of all self actualizing primates of being eaten and with the atmosphere of underlying dread so adequately described by our Aryan prophet, Mr Lovecraft. Baltimore is literally the east coast necropolis, where the filthy lies of merchant values, modernity, global capitalism and marxism ooze slime like and ever so slowly to its flesh dissolving conclusion. They didn't even have the excuse of being protestant! A century ago a prophet emerged from this place and wrote for The Baltimore Sun. Like most prophets he was ignored and later reviled.

His successor 100 years later writes on his computer in a rented room.

This book is NOT nihilistic or "might makes right" like it may appear to the shallow minded. It is quite human and touching with a respect and moral disgust underlying the chaos. I have read it at least eight times with many more future readings to come, but even near perfection has room for improvement. This was written nearly a decade and a half ago when James was not yet at his sage/hermit/recluse/prolific phase (who let this guy near a free publishing platform? Ha!). At this point, as seen on his blog (JamesLafond.com) he has distilled the essence of his street interactions and observations into some very useful and soon to be mandatory ways of conducting oneself in this shadowland we call the USA. I thought that an update with Jim's advice on how to conduct oneself when finding themselves on a concrete buffet table would help make the book more useful and dare I say, hopeful. Who says I am all doom and gloom? All joking aside. We are headed for dark days of anarcho-tyranny which has existed mainly at the fringes for the last few decades but now is spreading out, just like they want. All law abiding and I will be frank now, white people, will need the useful advice within these pages in the coming years. We are between the hammer of a cannibalizing and exploiting elite that has decided our kind needs to be slowly replaced and the anvil of a resentful and dysgenic lumpenprole population cultivated for that very purpose. The anti-white zeitgeist is becoming more explicit everywhere you look and the old NRA "muh guns" macho attitude is going to be used against you. Your outrage may be justified but it is useless. We are the Indians now. The demographic shifts are inevitable and long before the second amendment is overturned they are going to chew away at every pathway to it, effectively nullifying the whole thing. It is like James and Colin Flaherty, his kindred just up I-95, have been saying all along. They, the powers that be, don't give a damn about you and the violence committed against people like you is purposefully covered up every day in this corpse of a country by their media commissars. I have concluded that this place was aborted in the womb from the very beginning, paraphrasing Lothrop Stoddard who meant an entirely different country, but I understand others who are more well adjusted and honorable may not feel this way, fine. The good "america", the idealized version of it does exist. It exists in you and I don't want to see good people consumed by this monster and its many tentacles and spawn.

So where does LaFond's book fit in with all this? Avoidance and being unsavory to eat are at the crux of it. This is common self defense advice but rarely followed and is only ever really broached by so called experts in a very superficial way. Like a formality before going into impractical techniques or self serving macho war stories. James takes this to a whole deeper and dare I say, metaphysical level. In the end you want nothing to happen. You don't want things to get physical for myriad reasons and the only way to do this is the counterintuitive response of being a silent and an unknown quantity. The predators are you and you are them, we ALL fear the unknown. The most vicious psychopath in the dark reaches of his soul, has an oasis where sanity lingers and even he fears the unknown. For your honor as a man, for your sanity and that of your kin, for staying within and following the law whether we respect it or not, we must avoid the physical. Not at all costs but at 95% of it at least. Middle and working class white people and all decent non white people need to navigate this tight rope where the net below has been replaced with a shark tank. You must look and convey that you are unsavory, too tough or chewy, or maybe even poisonous. The near miss must be the width of a hair. You will feel and know fear. There is no escape from that, absolutely none. Life is a survival horror video game where you only have one life and no chance to restart it again.

You cannot separate history, culture, sociology, economics, gender, race and the power of irrationality from any of this. The Left, as vile as they are, are actually right for the wrong reasons. You need to know how you are viewed in the context of so many forces and powers that you have absolutely no control over. The red pill makes us all the doomed protagonists of a lovecraft tale of terror that NEVER ends. However letting go of the old delusion and becoming self aware is what James offers from his little cave in Baltimore. The line separating us and a hominid from the paleolithic period is quite fragile but we have a knowledge they could not possess. We have had nearly three centuries or more of this failed enlightenment experiment to see that we are limited beings, progress being a false castrating goddess. The shadows of the past when we huddled inside locked abodes at night, and shuddered at the sounds outside the perimeter are coming back. They never really left.

Goodnight, Ghouls and Boys...

Stay Sour!

Mescaline Franklin
First Day of Winter
2015

Dedication

For Tim "Uncle Nasty" Nolan, who was a good guy, and died in his sleep, on Friday, November 5th 2010, the same day he was interviewed for this book.

Author's Note

The material presented in this book is drawn exclusively from the author's own experience, and from interviews conducted between June 1996 and January 2011. Statistics are derived from those interviews documented between June 1996 and May 2000, which constitute 1675 documented acts of violence or aggression. 95% of these incidents took place in and around Baltimore Maryland. The names of victims, eye-witnesses and aggressors have been changed or altered unless that party requested otherwise.

The numbers preceding accounts come from my original violence index. **#23-16** would indicate that this account is found on page 23 of my graph paper index on line 16.

About the Author

James LaFond was born in 1963, and writes out of Northeast Baltimore City. He is a pedestrian, has lost 158 fights, has survived dozens of violent crimes, and enjoys jay-walking.

When You're Food

Mythic Reference

"I saw you in the fields when you were young,
I saw you graze with the wandering herds
but I did not kill you, you were too scrawny,
you would not have made a good meal...
...I will slit your throats,
I will cut off your heads, I will feed your reeking
guts to the screeching vultures and crows."

 -*The Epic of Gilgamesh*, adapted from the
2004 translation by Stephan Mitchell

When You're Food

Preface to the Advance Edition

My hard copy publisher is Paladin Press. They gave me my break and have treated me fairly. However, they, like other small publishers who issued predominantly trade paper backs have been hit hard by the publishing revolution and the reduction in literacy. However, though Paladin has agreed to publish the prequel to this book [*The Logic of Force*] they will not commit to this volume. I understand. But, they won't be in a position to give me an answer on *When You're Food* until after the apocalypse predicted by the ancient Mayan astronomers. I believe that when the Apocalypse comes in late December of this—possibly our last—year that the information contained in this book might be of some use to you and yours. The photos are poor quality copies of photocopies, because Paladin is sitting on the originals. If Paladin does decide to publish the book then this e-book version will be withdrawn from publication at that time.

In the meantime, you be safe out there.

-James LaFond, Friday January 13th 2012

Cutting to the Bone: The When You're Food Q&A

MF: If you only had a minute or two to tell someone who is about to go for a walk across Baltimore or Detroit or Newark how they should conduct themselves as to ensure their survival, what would you tell them? Assuming it's an able bodied man that you respect.

JL: Be the hunter, not the gatherer. The gatherer is the feminine. The hunter is the imaginative masculine. Imagine that you are going to kill or have just killed. You are the hunted hunter. In other words your body language should exhibit aspects of stalking. Imagine the police are looking for you while you are looking to kill somebody else. Aspects of this will be head on a swivel, no verbalization, no eye contact.

MF: Can you illuminate what you mean by the "imaginative masculine"?

JL: The ability to be able to imagine a variety of situations in a tactical format. Women generally lack an imaginative capacity. Their communication revolves around emotional reassurance and repetitive statement of fact. The mechanics of collecting fixed resources like bushes, roots, nuts and cultivating replacements. By contrast, the hunter must be able to imagine attacking, or being attacked by a variety of creatures in a possibly unknown setting. The implication of this for the survivalist is plain when one considers that the vast majority of men in civilized settings behave according to the female template described above. The people who do not behave in that manner are criminals, law enforcement and the military. You must think like one of these three types.

MF: So basically a female gathering berries has to see what is in front of her at that moment whereas a male hunter has to imagine many scenarios in his mind that may occur to maximize his chances of a successful kill. Also berries and nuts do not have fangs and claws or tomahawks. Is this the gist of it?

JL: Females are better at pattern recognition as evidenced by their dominance in proof reading, editing and facial recognition. Men make better writers. The primary skill of the champion athlete is pre imagining or visualizing clutch actions. By clutch action I mean the action, like a straight right hand or throw, that brings success. I don't like Ali but when you see photos of him throwing the right hand you can see in his eyes that he has imagined this countless times.

MF: Okay that makes a lot of sense. In regards to verbalization, how would this differ along gender lines and how is this applicable to our survival program?

JL: You must look at the behavior of a male population raised by women. In this book you will see many examples of a lone silent male facing down mobs of vociferous black males who behave like angry women. To fail in this situation all that is required of the individual is to behave like the aggressors. Then he is bitch in a bitch fight.

MF: What do you think the thought process, or more accurately the instincts, of these males raised by females is when faced by a silent male?

JL: Its chimpanzees dealing with a leopard. The first part is the need of the naturally insecure female to build consensus. The second is the need of the emasculated male to have justification for action. They are going to use repetitive language amongst themselves and with their antagonists to develop group cohesion and they are going to attempt to elicit a justifying action from the antagonist. An example is eliciting a racial slur from the target which will guarantee that collectively everyone in the group will act similarly and for the same unified purpose. So when the potential target says nothing they are left with an imagination inadequate to the task of divining the target's intention.

MF: So it is fear of the unknown in a nutshell?

JL: Yes! It's the leopard and the chimps again. During the day, the chimps will band together and drive the leopard off but at night they are all shivering and cringing in the trees. The leopard owns the night and night represents the fear of the unknown. My theory is our horrific monsters down through Dracula represent the leopard. So you want to bring the night aka the unknown with you.

MF: The night represents the unknown for the simple physical reason that primates cannot see too well in the dark. Leopards have heightened senses that enable them to operate and hunt in darkness. We have talked about the verbal, can we now talk about the visual?

When You're Food

JL: The frightened person, the prey, raises its head and makes wide eyes. The predator, the intent actionist has a narrow gaze. The middle ground where you can get caught is confrontational eye contact, a boxing stare down. You don't want this in a predatory scenario. If you think you are dealing with more than one aggressor you cannot devote all your focus to one. Narrow your eyes, look between the chin and the elbows. This keeps your prime targets in your field of vision and his weapons (hands and beltline).

MF: Okay we are looking thuggy, we are quiet, we are intent and swiveling our head to remain aware. What are we doing with our hands?

JL: At a distance you are swinging your hands and moving at an intentional pace, like you have somewhere to go. In proximity close in you want at least one concealed hand. It does not have to be in the pocket but they cannot have a clear view of both of your hands.

MF: What do you mean by swinging your hands?

JL: Your natural arm motions if you are walking like you have a destination and relaxed. Don't be tense or flexing like a tough guy. If somebody approaches you when you are walking intently it will be obvious, they will have to make an effort to make contact with you. I have avoided most trouble by walking at 5 miles per hour past people who think at 3 miles per hour. Now that he has approached you and it is obvious, then the concealing of one of your hands will be obvious to him if he has bad intentions.

MF: Okay here is the scenario, a quite common one. You are walking to your local pub to get a beer. There are three gentle giants in the proximity. Whether hanging out on the steps of an abandoned church you are passing or moving down the street in your direction by chance. How do you conduct yourself in the context of what we have discussed above? The overall tactical package of the "imaginative masculine".

JL: Most attacks are opportunistic not planned. To avoid them sensing an opportunity do not hesitate, do not divert your course around them, demonstrate awareness, move with intent, conceal one hand and walk on by without eye contact or verbal engagement.

MF: What if they don't move and you bump each other even slightly and you get that look and the "Yo! Why dont you say excuse me?!!"

SL: You have two courses depending on how you stack up to them.

Number one, bump through the group and if they follow you time your steps so you turn around and strike as he walks into it.

Number two, you walk by at a distance such that any bump is intentional on his part. He will either tighten ranks and move for you or he will spread out and go for the bump. If he goes for the bump you need to synchronize your steps so that your foot hits the sidewalk at the same time that his foot hits the sidewalk and your hand hits his chin.

MF: Okay the worse scenario. You are walking and being followed by three or more young men who are getting their lives back together. How do you deal with them at a distance? Then the nightmare scenario, how to deal when you get rushed?

SL: Number one, get something in your hand. A brick, a stone, a bottle, whatever. Number two start crossing the street diagonally looking over your shoulder and once you get on the other side stay on that side of the street. If they all cross the street behind you then cross again. If they cross again or rush you it's on. Rush the nearest guy. Get your back to a surface like a van or a wall and keep moving.

MF: Any miscellaneous observations before we wrap this up?

SL: Don't listen to what they say, your ears need to hear for footsteps and weapon deployment noises like a click.

MF: What if eye contact is made accidently as you turn a corner or something.

SL: Nodding is the courteous thing to do, you want to be polite. That cuts the confrontation out. Confrontations can be and must be avoided, so you can focus on predation.

Preface

I was scheduled to begin writing this book on January 2nd, 2011, but last night rendered that artifice obsolete, indeed turned my start-line into a self-imposed writer's block.

Between 1996 and 2000, when I wrote *The Fighting Edge* and *The Logic of Steel* I was living in Northeast Baltimore as a homeowner. In 2000 I completed the associated magazine articles and wrote the rough draft for the *Logic of Force* and this book, and began research for a history book. I then moved my family to a rental in Dundalk, a working class suburban enclave in Southeast Baltimore County, affectionately known by Tattoo Rick as "The Redneck Riviera." In 2004 I was fired by my wife, and fired twice more within 24 hours by two other women—a rare achievement that I remain proud of—and effectively became homeless for 6 weeks. From 2004 through 2010 I rented a room in North Baltimore County from a librarian, and spent most of that time managing a ghetto supermarket. This is the period when I wrote *The Broken Dance* volumes and re-wrote *The Logic of Force.*

I am currently renting a room in Northeast Baltimore, a 70% Black/30% White high-crime area with a negligible cultural signature. I am writing fulltime, which means I am poor. My roommate and I, a large karate instructor, generally leave the doors open. This practice, with medieval weapons lining the walls, makes this a Tower of Death, where the local criminals are invited to take their chances. If that makes Sensei upstairs Kareem Abdul Jabar, then I suppose I'm Dan Inosanto. Hopefully Bruce lee, looking for money to satisfy his craving for crack cocaine, doesn't show up while I'm taking my bath, because then I only have my scuba knife...

I manage not to starve by working as a part-time night grocer in the Middle River area of East Baltimore County. The event that triggered my early dive into this piece is detailed below.

To get to work at 8:30 p.m. I must leave my place at 7:10 p.m., walk one mile north, half way to the county line, take the #55 Bus for a 40-minute meandering ride east to Essex, and then walk a mile-and-a- half north to Middle River, a haven for bikers, construction workers and predominantly White welfare mothers and their snack-food and soft-drink consuming broods.

7:15 p.m., Monday, December 13th 2010

I was walking north on the west-side of Sefton. I crossed the street to the east side 150 yards ahead of a huge Dodge Ram pickup with gleaming chrome that rumbled like thunder coming down the street behind me from the south. This is the vehicle most commonly driven by gratuitous runt-stompers. As I was continuing my stroll down Sefton the truck rumbled up parallel with me and the passenger said, "Better stay out of our way asshole...kick your ass."

I did not look over at them and behaved as if I had not heard a thing, my standard response to runt stomping invitations which feature me as the runt. This same situation has been thrust upon me by at least three-dozen pairs or trios of White men driving pickup trucks over the previous two decades.

In the first portion of this book I will discuss the aspects of human-on-human predation.

The brief stillborn opportunity above for two sadists to enjoy the demise of some small old dude was easily avoidable so long as the old guy did not demonstrate any of the three most rational responses to this verbal setup for what I call psychological predation. Make no mistake, they treated me as food; not as flesh to be devoured, or property to be ill-gotten, but as a soul to be drained of self-worth, used to nourish their own vapid and powerless ghost of a collective soul through the beating and stomping of my material body and the drawing forth of the blood that maintains it.

If I had simply demonstrated fear; indignation or anger; all of which I felt as I questioned my ability to defend myself, bristled at the insult, and wondered if I should chew up and swallow the nose I would attempt to bite off in case of an attack, just out of spite, so that it could not be sewn back on. Thankfully my crooked ego and barbaric proclivities were sublimated beneath what have become automatic survival responses at this point in my life.

The old leopard made it back to his second-story den, and he imagines the two scrawny young lions prowling for more easy prey tonight, even as they skulk in abject and unmanning terror in the shadow of the larger, younger, more numerous, more ruthless, more fit, and yes **braver** lions that rule this city through a reign of terror: the young Black men of Baltimore.

We are all somewhere on a given food chain, with only a few of us ever being at or near the top. I hope you enjoy, or at least derive value from, the insight and ugliness ahead.

-James LaFond, Baltimore, Maryland, Tuesday, December 14th 2010

Chapter 1:

Being Hunted

"When I was young—jus' arrived in Baltimore from South Carolina—I joined a gang. There was all kind'a gangs. If you didn't belong to a gang you were up a crik. I suppose our best weapon was the bicycle chain looped ova en taped for a handle; that break some bones."
   -Israel

Since the dawn of man this is how our kind has instinctively protected themselves from predators; by banding into violent groups. Thus far, the modern nation state is the ultimate expression of the evolution of the violent group. I personally find this process to be infinitely dehumanizing, and have hence rejected it. I have never banded together with anyone for defense. Among other things, this made me a social aberration, a terrible football player, and as a teenager, something of a sociopath. It hasn't all been bad though. Being aberrant has provided me with a sense of freedom that others have often envied, and enough experience with avoiding violence and negotiating threats of violence from a mechanically and socially weak position to fill multiple books on the subject of personal violence.

In martial arts and self-defense scenarios the primary actor in every violent situation is the defender. In the real predatory world the primary actor in almost all violent situations is the aggressor. Let us therefore briefly empathize with the aggressor, so that we may be able to see violence from his perspective: the perspective that matters most to him; and should matter most to the usually ill-fated object of his attentions.   If you are a man, you are most likely primarily concerned with your ability to prevail in a social confrontation that escalates to physical contact: a fight.

This book is not about fighting. That is what I do for fun on Saturday morning. You can *always* avoid a fight [mutual combat]. If you chose to engage in a fight, my only concerns are: will I get to see it, and will it be entertaining? I am a big fight fan. I train fighters and I still compete in stick fights and machete duels. That may make me something of a nut. However, I have never permitted myself to be drawn into a fight outside of a sporting or dueling context since age 19. That is 29 years living as a pedestrian and working at night with alcoholics in one of the most dangerous cities in America. If I can avoid fighting, so can you.

60% of all violence is predatory. 98% of lethal violence is predatory. [The 2% of mutual combat deaths were tragic accidents.] What motivates a predatory aggressor? The answer is hunger. The only variable is that which he hungers for. When you have been singled out as prey, what hunger have you been designated to feed?

There are those few serial killers who are actually hungry to eat your flesh. This, of course, is a rare hunger in our age of factory farmed domestic animals. If you can predict what motivates the aggressor, than you have the key to deactivating him through positioning, body language and verbal actions. Ask yourself, "When he infringes upon my personal space, shatters my piece-of-mind, violates my rights, damages my body, rapes me, or even kills me, which of his ravenous needs has my demise nourished?"

Has the money he took from you fueled his crack addiction for yet another day? Has his wavering self-image been bolstered? Has his lack of self-esteem been temporary compensated for? Have his sadistic proclivities been satiated? Has his racial hatred been justified? Whether you have been targeted to feed his hunger for power, chemical addiction, self-esteem, perverse impulses or compelling hatred, at the moment of attack, you—your entire being—has been reduced to a consumable quantity. You have become food.

The people in this book either made it onto someone's menu, or count themselves among the potential connoisseurs of your misfortune.

Awareness Case-Studies

"...the idea of being attacked, of risking death that night in the dark streets of Thrax, lifted some part of the depression I would otherwise have felt."
-Gene Wolfe, *The Urth of The New Sun*

On Being Self-aware

Knowing, and being at peace with, how others view you, is a crucial aspect for assessing your own survival risks when dealing with predators, as well as your chances of success among civilized humans.

We must cultivate our self-awareness, even—or especially when—it hurts to do so. Last night my former girlfriend called—just to remind me that I was, and would always be, an "asshole". I cringe to think that I am, and am for ever fated to be, in social terms, the aforementioned orifice. I must admit though, that I am occasionally just that.

As a supermarket manager I fired 85 night crew clerks, janitors and cashiers in a four year period. I only had one of these guys slug me. The other guy actually missed—and I was looking the other way! In any case, I quickly cultivated the reputation as an unwavering enforcer of rules. The upside is that this is good for morale. The downside is that this makes you completely predictable.

Toby, a likeable smart-ass college student, wanted to party. Toby could not afford to call out again or he would be suspended. He hatched a brilliant plan to get sent home for violating dress code and the cell-phone policy. There I find him, manning register #8, texting on his cell, jamming out to the tunes pulsating from his I-pod—plugged into *my* power source—and wearing shorts and sleeveless-T in early April! Surely, the draconian management functionary would send him home?

I toyed with him, passing him by on numerous occasions, pretending not to notice the shorts, the music. Each time I came by, he was a little more obvious with his texting, the hairy leg stuck out into the lane a little farther, the heavy metal blared a little louder. Eventually I unleashed my trademark of pending-cashier-doom: I bagged his customer's order and then slowly reached across his line of sight and turned off his register light. I then produced the three documents, the litany of his crimes against *Ghetto Grocer Inc.* on that day. He barely managed to repress a smile as he was served, "Toby, I would gladly send you home and bank the saved payroll to add to my bonus while I work your coworkers to death to make up for your well-deserved absence. But, I just had to send my frozen food man home for a dress code infraction [wearing a hooded sweatshirt on the sales floor]. Come with me."

When You're Food

Toby meekly followed me back into my former hellish domain where I had worked for 15 years, as a frozen food clerk. As we stepped into the ancient roaring walk-in, which did not shut off when the door opened, and remained a nippy 15-below [not factoring the wind-chill], I informed him that the stock in this box would have to be moved to another box. He was already shivering. We next entered the ice-cream walk-in, where 9 humming fans kept the temperature at 30-below, "Now Toby, all of the stock on this wall, goes to this empty wall. Then all of the stock from the other box comes to this wall—that's called product rotation."

While returning to the sales floor, I came face-to-face with Ty—who was bringing a pair of gloves for Toby—the spitting image of heavyweight contender Michael Grant, "Ooh Jimmy, if I say it you'll have ta send me home, so I'll jus' leave it alone."

Well, my former girl said it for him. Suffice it to say, that I tend to extremes. In the year 2000, as I was closing in on wrapping up the *Violence Project*, I had even taken to wandering dimly lit streets and alleys in the worst parts of town, hoping to be attacked so that I would generate more material for my work. It never happened though, so I gave that up, just assuming that my research had somehow resulted in me developing a mugger-repellent aura. I was now stumbling through life without self-awareness, forgetting that my dubious activities had attracted the attention of Fate, a most jealous wife...

MaraChrismas Yo
Christmas Eve, December 24th, 2000, 10:00 PM, Locust Point, South Baltimore

I leave the supermarket I work at as a night clerk. The manager let us pull a 6:00 p.m. to 10:00 p.m. shift. Of course, being an asshole, I told the wife I was working 6:00 p.m. to 12:00 a.m. so that I could take advantage of an invitation to visit a smoking-hot rich chick that lived on the other side of Riverside Park. She was a snob, so I decided to spare her that sinking feeling she must have gotten in her stomach every time she watched me get dressed, and came face-to-face with the fact that she was receiving DNA from a guy who dressed like a bum.

Merry Christmas Baby, I'm not really an evolutionary dead-end!

So I walk off into the cold gusty night pulling on the heavy woolen gloves I would never trust in a fight, in a dress coat rather than the duster, and protecting my head with a wool cap that warms the ears rather than the twisted rag I normally wore. I am even wearing the scarf my mother knitted for me in 1972! I'm breaking all the rules of survival attire for my mistress...and Charles Darwin is watching...

As I cut through Riverside Park I spot three young men drinking and headed my way. I cut across the grass to avoid a potential confrontation and run into a rich dude walking his dog. It is after dark in a city park. We are all breaking the law.

I emerge from the canine latrine known as Riverside Park, and head down Barney. As I cross Charles Street, a large muscular man crosses in my direction. I pull off my right glove to get a tissue. He glances uneasily at my concealed hand and steps wide to my left and hurries on as we pass.

10:15 p.m., Hanover Street

My girl lets me into her place, and I see that her ankle is in a cast. A slip on the ice I think. Even I'm not such an animal to take advantage of her in this condition, so I get her upstairs to bed, fix her a cocktail and snacks and sit and talk for an hour or so. She mentions that I look pale and washed out. I assure her that I am not sick. I had just been up for 52 hours and was on a powerful muscle-relaxer because I had not taken the time to stretch-out my hip-rotators and hams...and the broken thumb was nearly healed... She chided me once again for stick-fighting and boxing. We then read nursery rhymes for about a half hour. Look, if you are a child, or are built like Scarlet Johansen, I will read nursery rhymes to you, okay.

Christmas Morning, 12:04 a.m., Hanover & Light

As I rise to leave she says, "You be careful out there. There's nothing but bad out there this time of night." She looks worried and that sends a shiver up my spine. I lingered a little too long so I have to run every second block if I'm going to catch the 12:15 bus at the Inner Harbor.

12:08 p.m., Hanover & Cross

A man emerges from an alley behind a liquor store with a case of vodka. He whispers, "Six fifths for twenty bucks."

I respond, "Nah man", and sprint the next block, sure that the cops will soon be descending on this corner.

12:20 a.m., Light & Pratt

I board the #10 Bus to Dundalk Center. There are about seven of us losers on this bus. A young white man with a backpack full of beer bottles steps nervously onto the bus and inquires about his destination by neighborhood. The driver just knows the route according to stops, and I'm too much of a Darwinian prick to help him out. The Mexican dudes don't care. But the old black drunk dude does, "Yo, I getcha dare fo a drink."

These two start drinking together as I begin to dose off and a pretty black girl gets on...

12:40 a.m., Dundalk & Holabird

At this stage in my life I'm working 48 hours a week, reading at a private library 40 hours a week, training 20 hours a week, spending 6 hours a week as the rich girl's houseboy, and spending the balance of my time in transit, playing army men with my 11-year-old son, and writing violence books. I have no idea why my wife is always pissed.

When You're Food

I get most of my sleep—about 2 hours a day—on the bus. My brain is wired to wake me when the bus stops; a full-proof system so long as I'm not the only bus patron. This night I have the good fortune of riding with the pretty young girl who happened to be getting off at Holabird and Dundalk, within sight of the county line—almost out of the war-zone.

I lurch off the bus behind her, half asleep, as a veritable United Nations all-star team of thugs greets her with catcalls: a black middle-weight; a black welterweight; a white-trash welterweight; and a Latino lightweight. When they see me the catcalls turn to threats as they wolf and posture at my expense and for her benefit. I do not listen to what they say and simply yawn and walk across the street with my eyes closed so I can tune my ears in and let my eyes adjust to the dark ahead. All the businesses are closed. As I walk up Holabird past Sensei Grosscup's Dojo and open my eyes I catch no sight of the thugs off behind me.

12:43 a.m., Holabird & Sollers Point

I hear a cough 2 blocks to my rear. That seems strange, since no one got off the bus behind me, and suburbanites, unlike city-dwellers, rarely walk anywhere, particularly at night. I pick up my pace and try to key up my hearing, but the gusting wind is making it tough to pick out anything. When I think I am being followed I never stop and turn unless I am heavily armed, and all I have is a razor. Despite the tension I am still nodding off; falling into micro-naps.

12:45 a.m., Holabird & Tolson

I hear the scuff of a shoe 1 block to my rear. I'm a fast walker who puts in 10 miles a day. This guy is either tall or he is trying to close the distance. I cut diagonally to the left across the street, glancing over my left shoulder as I step off the curb. I catch movement in a doorway 50 yards to my rear

12:47 a.m., Holabird & Crafton

As I continue my brisk walk on the left side of Holabird I hear someone step off the curb behind me. The only open business on this stretch is Phillip's Inn, a half-block ahead. This guy is either headed there or is going to whack me down the road. I consider stopping in to shake the pursuit, if, in fact, I am being pursued. I decide against ducking into the bar because: I've never been there and the fat hillbillies in Dundalk are generally hostile to me; I'm too tired to have another drink without impairing my already diminished physical ability and mental acuity; and I won't be herded into a hole from which I must pop up at 2:00 AM. I roll the dice in my mind and pass the bar.

12:48 a.m., Passing Phillip's Inn toward Snyder

Though I'm listening for the bar door to open and shut, the heavy winds are interfering with my hearing. Am I clear?

12:49 a.m., Holabird & Snyder

The sidewalk ends for a block as it turns into a grassy brush-covered median strip separating Holabird and Maple [a parallel service road]. As I step off the curb I elect to risk oncoming traffic [of which there is presently none] on the poorly lit main road, instead of walking down Maple in the dark. I walk down Holabird five feet from the curb and ten feet from the center line.

12:49 a.m., Holabird & Cedar—almost

Just as a heavy gust of wind dies down I hear the scratchy plastic sound of puffy nylon sleeves brushing against the body of a coat. I look over my left shoulder to see the oppressed middleweight from Dundalk Avenue bearing down on me in full stride. He is tall, sprinting in good form, knees pumping above the waist, and almost 20 yards back. He will hit me in two seconds, four seconds if I try to run.

His partner, the lightweight Spanish kid in the hoody, is flanking me on the left coming up the gutter on this side of the median, ten yards back and four feet out. He is even faster than the brother. I want desperately to kill this twerp. But every horrible scenario that flashes through my mind [This is when you are supposed to have the good visions out of your past flash before your eyes.] has me and this big lead-paint-eating knuckle-dragger taking all the damage. I hate the Spanish kid mostly because he is more cunning and bolder than I am. I'll just have to take it out on his hitter.

When You're Food

As this witch's brew of angst percolates within my damaged brain I am already working my drill: shucking the glove into the coat pocket; lifting the coat flap; sliding out the box-cutter; and deploying it by hitting the butt against my hip. [I still remember that feeling ten years later.] I begin to extend my left hand for a grab with a slight reverse-pivot to my right into the street—hoping that some drunk in a pick-up truck will splatter us both, leaving the little mastermind here to search through the gore for the two dollar bills remaining in my wallet...

The knuckle-dragger isn't just some welfare sucking opportunist. He is willing to crash into me face first and keeps pumping those legs even as his eyes grow wide with fear. I experience an inappropriate erection. [This is not something I am proud of, but something which, in keeping with the subtext of this chapter, I feel compelled to disclose.] I am thinking to myself, 'Three steps homeboy and we're blood-brothers.'

Two long strides from the realization of my dark blood-drenched fantasy I hear the Spanish guy, "Woah, yo, woah—he got sometin'!"

They both break to their left as big-boy breaks his stride. I'm now calling them Beefy and The Brain in my mind. Beefy's eyes are as big as jumbo eggs as he sucks in cold air. He and The Brain continue flanking me at a fast walk, trying to cut across my route. The Brain has his right hand in the pocket of his hoody, "Whachyo gonna pull a gun on us man?"

I continue to back up. My mind tells me to keep quiet. My body tells me to scream and charge, because I now believe he has a knife. What emerges from me is an unconscious compromise; an incoherent snarl as I continue to back down the street, edging away from them toward the center slightly. I suddenly become aware that cops might come by and that I don't want to be seen holding a weapon, so I slide my blade hand up into the coat pocket and continue backing away.

As they persist in flanking me The Brain continues, "Woah, yo—Main Man, whachyou pull a gun on us fo? We wadn't comein' up on chyou or nuttin'.

Inhuman snarl from the bum disguised as a lawyer.

"Yo yo muthafuca, whachyo problem?!?"

I begin calculating. Does he want a fight now, having decided that I also have a blade? Or is he just wolfing to save face with his muscle? After all, this was obviously his ingenious plot to relieve me of my last two dollars?

They vanish immediately back down Maple and I turn to walk forward and put some distance between us. Just then an SUV doing about 70 flicks on its beams and blows by me, brushing my coat sleeve with its mirror. Yes, The Brain saw the truck flying toward me without its lights on, piloted by a drunk from Howards Pub a half-mile ahead.

1:10 a.m., Wise and Lynch

My dark fantasy came close to coming true. Not close enough though. I am five minutes from my boy's Christmas tree and the toy display I am going to set up underneath of it—for possibly the last Christmas he will actually want toys.

I owe a debt to those two predators that hunted me ten years ago. The light side of my mind was reminded that I should have already been home with my neglected wife. The dark side of my mind was given another justification for its existence. For me, being hunted by those scumbags was another small step toward becoming a whole person.

God Can Certainly Count to Four

A Wednesday, March 2001, 2:30 p.m., North Boundary Road, Dundalk, Baltimore County

I expressed the onset of my mid-life crisis, and my worry over the rapid deterioration of my already modest boxing ability, by becoming involved in full-contact stick-fighting. The ironic thing about stick-fighting is that the constant broken, sprained and swollen hands that result make practical self-defense pretty difficult. At this stage, about 200 fights into my dubious career, I typically could not make a fist and lacked the manual dexterity to deploy a razor. I had decided therefore that I would use an ink pen for self defense, and, when hauling my gear, use my helmet as a flail if assaulted.

When You're Food

On this particular day I'm walking east on North Boundary, five minutes from my humble abode, a case of sticks in my right hand, a helmet with gloves inside of it in my left. Walking parallel with me on the other side of the street, in front of the post-modern church, is a tall attractive girl in her early teens, coming home from school. Cruising alongside her are four high school seniors, who appear by their build to be football players. The passenger is speaking obscenities to the girl, who is nervous. He even mentions that they plan on "gang-banging" her.

Her stride is becoming meek as she quakes and becomes openly fearful. I will soon outpace her. If she were a male I would just walk on. But she is a girl. I can't even stand watching movies were girls get killed. I stop as she stops. At this point the four young studs, who appear to range around 5' 10" and 200 pounds, notice me noticing them. The passenger actually produces a megaphone, arcs his body up out of the car, and yells a threat over the roof at me as the driver speeds off. I am feeling arrogant. So I stand proudly and give them the finger, something that I have never done, and it feels good!

The driver puts his mother's rice-burner into reverse and they speed back toward me, pulling up about ten yards away. As all four doors are thrown open every boy except the driver piles out with a baseball bat in hand. I drop my case and go to one knee, draw my heavy stick from the side slot, dump the gloves out of the helmet, and shove the unbuckled shell onto my head as I rise. They should be at long-hand range by now. Unfortunately, they are all piling back into the car, which speeds off. I am left feeling like the geek who showed up at the neighborhood football game on Christmas morning, with his brand new football, only to have the other kids leave for home like he was some kind of leper. [Yes, that really happened to me when I was eight-years-old.] I spread my arms and yell, "Guys! Come on back!"

To tell the truth, I think I spiked my helmet in anger and disappointment. Only the girl would know for sure. She was being hunted. I was just an asshole looking for a fight. Somehow it all worked out. I hope she has enjoyed a happy life and has put this experience in perspective. I hope those four jocks ran head-on into a dump-truck.

How might your perspective on being hunted differ from situation to situation? Much depends on your nature, your options, and some variables way beyond your control.

Photo #1: A typical approach posture by a lone armed predator. The weapon is usually concealed or refused, not presented or brandished. If it's looking like this, it's for keeps.

Chapter 2

Elements of Human-on-Human predation

"When an Indian is killed, it is a great loss which leaves a gap in our people and a sorrow in our heart. When a White is killed, three or four others step up to take his place and there is no end to it."
-Chiksika, March 19th, 1779

Being physically violated without managing a potent or even credible defense, or at least a counterattack, is to be plunged into the deepest well of powerlessness. I have known this since childhood. On the first day of my first-grade year at Immaculate Heart of Mary I was attacked, beaten, and thrown to the ground repeatedly by three second-graders, simply for their amusement. I was just a fat little person crying as my tormentors savored my despair. I was soon rescued by Chris, an aggressive third-grader, who became like a big-brother to me until I attained the heights of puberty and morphed into a creature far more violent than the three who had begun my education.

Our physical autonomy is at the core of our sense of freedom, even our individuality. The most common, and most potent, threats to our person stem from our association with, and alienation from, various social organisms, or groups.

When Suzy, a white girl, was mugged by two black men on Parkside Drive, it was her gender and race, and their gender and race that put her at risk. The predators were instinctively drawn to her as physically vulnerable [female] prey. The justification for their actions—which all but the purest predators require—came from her obvious membership in a more powerful group, responsible for their group's oppression.

Below is the predation check list, the partially subconscious process by which human predators select human prey. Every time the predator answers yes to any of the following questions that are asked of him by his primal nature, the likely-hood that he will attack, increases. This is in effect a progressive list of pre-conditions.

Pre-conditions for Predation

1. Is he a superior [bigger, harder, stronger, better armed] force?
2. Is the prey alone?
3. Is the prey isolated [no potentially hostile witnesses or allies]?
4. Is the prey a member of an alien group?
5. Is he acting as part of a group?
6. Is he acting as part of an agitated [drunk, high, hate-filled] group?
7. Is he acting as part of a high-cohesion group?

Note, that every one of these pre-conditions is a risk-limiting factor. Your hunter begins his assessment of your palatability by weighing his chances of overcoming you. This always begins as an individual assessment. Each member of a potential group of attackers will individually measure themselves against the target. This will remain the primary factor in their success projection unless the group is agitated or of high-cohesion. After the predator has weighed his chances of success his concern shifts to his chances of avoiding repercussions. The most potent predatory force in the equation is unseen: an army of heavily-armed high-cohesion aggressors, *the police*. The equation favors group action: increasing the attacker's chances of success, limiting his physical risk, *and* legal risk. Groups are far more likely to attack than individuals. The likely-hood further increases as the size of the immediate group increases.

Photo #2: Action typical of a high-cohesion group attack.

When You're Food

Alienation, A Case Study: Riding The #10 Bus with Dave the Electrician, April, 1996

I am waiting for the bus with a man that looks familiar. It turns out to be Dave. Dave had been wiring the lighting for the grand opening of a supermarket I was stocking back in 1993 when he got deathly ill and went home sick. A half-hour later he called us up and said he was waiting for the cops to come lock him up.

I am watching two would be hip-hop honeys in tight jeans, tube-tops and denim vests dancing under the bus shelter when Dave approaches me and nods as if at a museum exhibit, "A Fugin' matin' dance I assume. They're breedin' like rats. These two 'ill be poppin' out drug dealers by next year."

We piled on the bus between some Mexicans and blacks and an Asian kid. I asked him how long he had been out of prison...

"I'm headed for my piss-test; a condition of my probation. The judge was pretty cool; a broad. She told my wife that she was lucky; that if it had been her old man he would have shot her too. You know, I could have cared less who the slut was screwing. But I was tired, and the guy was in my bed. He was a big East Side prick—young. She told 'im not to give me any shit. She knew.

I told him to leave, and he told me to go to Hell! I reached under the mattress and pulled out my forty-five, and he still wouldn't go. He actually threatened me, in my house, in my bed! When I put it behind his knee I knew it was going to ruin his night. But I didn't expect the whole knee cap to go flying across the room! Just like that [Dave makes a low outward arc with his open right hand.) kind'a slow. Since he threatened me I just had to pay for the knee cap and do the time for the firearms charge. The time wasn't so bad.

But this, takin' the bus, I can't stand it. I was in Nam, saw combat. It wasn't that bad. A lot a guys whine about it. But it at least made sense. Not like this bullshit in The States (Dave shakes head and nods toward homeboy listening to rap on his headset.) Over there, out in the field, if it was yellow you shot it. You come back here and look at this shit (Dave makes a sweeping backhand motion toward the many uncomfortable bus patrons in our area of the coach.) What the fuck is this? The United Nations? Who's the enemy over here?"

Dave now makes a pistol barrel and hammer out of the index finger and thumb of his right hand and begins pointing at individual passengers and pressing his thumb forward as he digresses, "Look: black; brown; yellow; red; white-without-shoes—what-the-Hell-kinda-Spic is that anyhow? I've had it with this political correctness. Take it easy pal—my stop."

As the back door of the bus slams shut my fellow bus patrons breathe a collective sigh of relief. One young black girl cannot take her eyes off of Dave, walking off in the gathering April rain with his hands in the pockets of his olive-drab bomber jacket.

Why did I introduce you to Dave? Because Dave's casual attitude towards lethal force and his intolerance towards members of other social groups remains a cautionary tale. Whatever group you appear to be part of, those who shall seek to separate you from your money, sense-of security, or your body will inevitably view you as callously as Dave did our fellow bus patrons on that chilly rainy day.

Those who prey upon you need to be able to easily identify you as "other" or "outsider" at the very least, though preferably as an actual member of an enemy group. It is not always enough that you be an enemy. You must also—particularly in cases of extreme violence—be perceived as an aspect of a social imbalance that places this person's entire extended family and way-of-life in jeopardy.

Always remember, that even the bad guy has a deep need to feel like the good guy. Almost nobody, wakes up, looks in the mirror, and thinks, "Yeah, that guy is evil."

Some Basic Equations

Below are some basic examples of predatory incidents from this study. Much of the statistical base comes from such very brief one-dimensional attacks. The first number indicates the page this incident is recorded on in my graph-paper index. The second number indicates the line. Each incident had to feature eight confirmable bits of information to be included in the study. Up to 48 pieces of information could be packed onto a single line entry by the use of symbols, coloring and bisected boxes.

Eugene
#16-19; night, seconds, first-person defender

"I was leaving Johnny's place [a city bar], headin' down the sidewalk within the fifty feet for loiterin' when these three guys approached me in a semi-circle. The one on my left—their right—was nearest to the building. He pulled a revolver and held it low pointed at my chest. That was the dude that did the taking. The others were just helpers. The guys says, "Give me yo money—en da chain."

I gave my chain to the middle guy and handed my money to the guy on my right. They just walked off, west across Paterson park, I guess to buy their drugs."

Bryant
#13-14: night, seconds, first-person defender

"Dawn and I had been at the Baha [a night club]. We had a lot to drink and I had walked her home. I was walking down Light Street past the antique shop and the gyro stand—staggering straight on. I heard a step behind me and something slammed me across the back, just below the shoulder blades. I dropped right to my knees. I was drunk as shit.

I looked back over my shoulder and seen this colored guy standing over me with a board in his hands—cocked for a swing. I didn't think. I just mule kicked him. (Bryant, a middleweight kick-boxer, demonstrates a back-kick from one knee while pushing off with his hands.) I caught him right under the ribs with the heel of the cowboy boot and he went down.

I got up on my feet and looked down at the guy. He's gasping for air. I kept looking at him while I picked up the board—a two-by-four. After I picked the board up I kept walking. I made a left on Fort Avenue and got up to the funeral home before I looked down and realized I was still carrying the board. I remember standing on the sidewalk just holding this thing. Then I dropped it and walked on home.

Walking the streets at night when you are that drunk is taking an unnecessary risk. I should have spotted the guy. It's not like he came at me out of a doorway or from behind a car. I wasn't even crossing the street. He just walked straight up on me and I was oblivious to his approach."

Both Eugene and Bryant were selected as prey after multiple calculations on the part of those who literally hunted them. Eugene was approached by his attackers outside of a bar in much the same way as lions would converge on an ungulate leaving a watering hole they were stalking. His hunters were organized, cohesive, had a plan, divided tasks among themselves, and only expended the effort necessary to secure what they sought. Bryant's attacker singled out a drunk, armed himself, and approached stealthily from behind in the dark, and pounced like a leopard on his unsuspecting prey. If Bryant had not possessed a potent counterattack in the form of his booted kick, he could have been severely injured. It is common for a loan predator to use more force than a group when committing a for-profit crime such as a robbery or mugging.

Chapter 3

Social Mechanics of Mass Aggression

A group is a living social organism with a life-span tied to its level of cohesion. The more cohesive a group, the more long-lived and potent it will be. Military and law-enforcement units and sports teams are clear examples of high-cohesion groups. The cohesion level of formal criminal groups varies widely. The cohesion of informal civil and criminal groups is usually dismal, with siblings raised in violent households being a notable exception. Below is a primer on informal criminal groups; their nature and functional components.

Cohesion

The level of cohesion of a violent group is far more indicative of its lethality than is its size.

Crowds: A typical crowd might consist of loosely associated drunks brought together by their shared affection for their favorite sports team. A crowd will usually consist of a lot of mouth* and meat*, and tend to be short on muscle*. If a crowd is big enough though, it will be deadly.

Cliques: A typical clique might be a gang "set". The individuals in this group will have a shared identity, shared hatreds, and shared goals. A clique will tend to be balanced, and will rarely coalesce for action without the presence of significant muscle within its ranks. There will be at least one unconditionally dangerous actor in this group.

Packs: This is a clique consisting of experienced actors, who will tend to use planning, and may even have engaged in some type of rudimentary training. Criminal dept collectors, enforcers, and bouncers qualify as packs under this definition.

Function*

A member of a violent informal group will serve one or more [usually just one] of the following functions. Leadership is defined here as a trait, not as a function.

Meat: This person is usually just a hanger-on, rarely a leader. He lends emotional support to the active members of the group. This is the guy who kicks you when you are down.

Muscle: For significant violent action to occur at least one individual must be physically dangerous or armed, and have the mind-set necessary to engage in close-proximity violence. This person may, or may not, be in a leadership position. It is, however, very unlikely that he is also running his mouth.

Mouth: This person might be a leader, a follower, bait, an assigned instigator, a spokesperson, or a cheerleader. Be careful not to focus on him or her, because their function is generally to set you up for action by another more lethal member of the group

Photo #3: Scene of a 7-on-2 fatal pack attack. Only 1 attacker was prosecuted, doing 6 months. Since the victim died from drowning rather than directly from the force of a blow, murder charges were not brought. The adult [muscle] members of the pack—pretending to be witnesses—successfully portrayed their crime as a mutual combat between the victim and one of their adolescent [meat] side-kicks.

A Clique Function Case-Study: Yo Rambo, Show Us Yo Gun

A Thursday, May, 1993, 9:00 a.m., Highland Ave. & Baltimore Street, Highland Town, East Baltimore

I transfer from the #23 Bus coming into town from the County and board the #22 Bus heading out of East Baltimore into Northeast Baltimore. As the driver clips my transfer ticket I am struck by a deafening din coming from the back of the bus. The driver looks up into my eyes, "Don't do anything stupid white-boy."

The front seats are occupied by perhaps a dozen elderly and invalid persons, some of whom are literally hunched forward, ducking the raging sounds of unbridled adolescence roaring through the bus as if the sound were the downdraft of helicopter rotor blades. Behind the last elderly woman, well prepared for a shopping expedition with her 20-pound purse and two-wheel dolly-basket, is a stretch of unoccupied seats three-deep.

As the bus pulls off I look up past no-man's-land and am greeted by eight suddenly silent faces; some staring, some glaring, waiting for me to surrender to their menacing presence and sit down in front of them. They should be in school by now, but it is a nice day, and now it is hooky time. They are 14 to 17-years-old, all featherweights and lightweights dressed in shorts, sneakers and tank-tops, with one exception.

He is a thick cruiserweight in baggy jeans, hat, and knit West African style jacket. He is sitting on the back bench seat—hands in pockets—one seat from the right corner; a good spot, not the best. He is the hitter, not taking his eyes off of the handbag in my right hand, which holds my hammer, screw-driver, lunch-bag, 12-inch Othello fighting knife, and head-rag. No eye-contact. He is strong and armed. If they attack I have to kill him quickly. I need to get close.

Four featherweights are stretched out in front of the back door. I walk by them. Two tall lightweights lay on the side bench seats behind the door. There is a nervous little guy sitting in the back right corner. He's out of the equation.

The silence persists as I walk past the trouble makers. I have a utility knife behind my belt buckle obscured by the flannel shirt wrapped around my waist. I lift the feet of the lightweight on the right-side [my left] bench and toss them into the aisle. This brings a gasp from the boys, a glare from the driver, and a nod of approval from the hitter, who appreciates me recognizing his status. It is clear to all that I want to sit next to him. I nod back at him and decide to trap his right hand in his pocket with my left while I slice open his throat.

The bus rolls and a half-empty can of soda whirls by my face and almost hits the hitter. I scan the faces of the punks ahead and put my hand into my handbag as the bus heads up Edison Highway. An amazing thing now happens: a hip-hop concert is arranged and executed in my honor, with all but the hitter participating. The elderly patrons cringe in horror. The bus driver looks at me in his mirror and shakes his head in disgust. I sit back and relax.

The rhythm section begins in honor of the enemy warrior:
clap, double-handed thigh slap, foot-stomp...

The shortest featherweight leaps up and begins twisting, spinning, shuffle-stepping and clapping in time, as seven voices begin a chant I shall never forget:

"Yo" clap, slap, stomp
"Rambo" clap, slap, stomp
"Show us" clap, slap, stomp
"Yo gun" clap, slap, stomp...

These kids can sing. I am entertained. The dancer advances to the door and begins to strip off his shirt as he continues to cavort and gyrate:

"Yo" clap, slap, stomp
"Rambo" clap, slap, stomp
"Show us" clap, slap, stomp
"Yo gun" clap, slap, stomp...

They all begin to sway frantically, destabilizing the bus as it reels across the bridge over the railroad tracks. The driver is pissed! The dancer is now gyrating before me and the local war-chief; kings of this savage little world. At about this time a locker-room scene flashes before my eyes and I realize that they don't want me to show them the UZI they believe to be in my handbag. But the less imposing instrument of genetic terror housed within my jeans. The boy is dancing ever more furiously, even doing an American split in the aisle and popping back up into a spin:

"Yo" clap, slap, stomp
"Rambo" clap, slap, stomp
"Show us" clap, slap, stomp
"Yo gun!" clap, slap, stomp...

As the bus sways the dancer spins on his toes and turns down the waist-band of his shorts to present his "gun". The hitter and I avert our eyes at the proper moment. I smile and nudge him, "I knew you weren't with these guys."

He nods, smiles and takes his hands from his pockets and intertwines his fingers on his lap. I remove my hand from my bag. Primary group cohesion disrupted.

All seven of the war-chief's entourage rise, grab the overhead bars and door-handles, and begin rocking the bus. The chorus resumes, with the rhythm now provided exclusively by stomps:

"Yo" stomp, stomp, stomp
"Rambo" stomp, stomp, stomp
"Show us" stomp, stomp, stomp
"Yo gun!" stomp, stomp, stomp

The bus is now in danger of tipping so the driver stops and the hitter rises and steps toward the door. Just then the door opens, 200 hundred yards short of a stop, and a soda can whips by my face, getting a little bit of cola on my chin. Satisfied with the performance I reach into my bag to get a rag to wipe off my chin. When the seven young men see my hand go into the bag they rush the door, become jammed in its mouth, and the bus begins to tip. I decide to have some fun and do not withdraw the rag but instead rotate my hand within the bag as if I am selecting some instrument of dread. They panic and rush through the jammed door, two bodies caught at awkward angles.

The hitter remains calm above and behind them. But the seventh boy in line is the nervous little kid from the back right corner. He is shaking as he looks at me in terror. As I fix him with an icy stare a tear begins to streak down his cheek and he says, "Please mister, please..."

One of the jammed bodies pops loose and they are all sucked out of the door. The driver mumbles something and the crippled guy by the front door laughs as I wipe off my face.

The next morning is chilly, with a windy overcast sky. The rain has not come yet, but windshield wipers are swishing away as motorists cross Highland on Baltimore in a whirlwind of flying newspapers, sub wrappers and supermarket circulars. I board the #22 Bus, driven by a large black woman this day. There is a single passenger sitting on the back left bench seat. It is one of the tall lightweights from yesterday. He is dressed in jeans and a tank top and is obviously chilly. I sit across from him and he avoids eye-contact. As the bus heads up Edison Highway I draw a razor and begin trimming my fingernails. He is a Belair-Edison Boy and is two miles from his stop. He gets off just before the bridge and walks home as the rain begins to fall.

That was a high cohesion, but not mission oriented, group: a clique. There was plenty of meat and mouth, but only one muscle. There was also no apparent leadership. I enjoyed the show. Thanks guys.

What follows is a take from my past that features the morphing of a violent group from a clique, to a crowd, and then into a pack, as it interacts with an individual, a pack, and an individual.

The Many-Headed Beast
1995, Springtime in Northeast Baltimore's brownstone ghetto

Jerad, my 18-year-old son, was buying cigarettes at the Korean liquor store when a mixed-race group of younger teens demanded his money. He hit one, ran, lost his hat in the process, and made it to the safety of our house. His two friends, Jake and Darrin, decided to go punish these punks. The punks fled down Belair Road [U.S. Route #1] to their neighborhood [Belair-Edison] and returned with about 8 more punks, including two obnoxious screaming girls. I have yet to be informed of this.

When You're Food

5:45 p.m, Tuesday

Jerad, Jake and Darrin are hanging out in front of the house talking loud enough to keep me awake. I open the window and lean out, "Hey, I have to get up for work in two hours. Keep it down."

6:15 p.m.

I wake to a thundering crash; like a storm-door being kicked in. I roll out of bed and lurch to my feet toward the window, banging my forehead on the window frame.

Jake and Darrin are squared off against a mob: an ugly cussing black girl; a fat screaming blood-thirsty white-girl; a big black boy; a tall skinny white-boy; and eight skinny black boys with sticks. [Jerad had been sent back to the house by Jake and was not in sight.] My five-year-old, Garren, is pushing his toy police car around in the yard declaring that everyone is under arrest. His mother is standing on the porch yelling for the mob to leave. [I found out later that three of our neighbors had called 911. The police never came.]

I grab my bowie knife and something hits my leg. I stop for a few seconds to put on a jock-strap, banging my forehead on the dresser, tripping over the floor fan and falling into the bookshelf. I run down the stairs, bounce off the wall and slam into the storm-door face first. I hit the safety glass with enough force that the whole crowd turns and looks in my direction: a mostly naked sawed-off Ted Nugent with a knife.

Jake looks at me with big eyes and motions for me to stay back, apparently more concerned for my embarrassment than his safety. He charges the crowd, hits a couple, and disperses and chases them down the street, having his leg cut by a swung stick in the process.

Dave, the retired cop across the street, says, "Those girls will drive them back here by tomorrow with some real hitters. The cops will be at least a half-hour getting here if they come at all. You don't want them getting in the house, and if you stop them in the yard with that fucking thing you are going to prison. Get a night-stick."

8:00 p.m. Tuesday to 4:00 p.m. Wednesday

I work the night job in the city, work the day job in the county, and head back downtown to the martial arts supply store and buy a 31-inch-long, 1-inch-thick, iron-wood stick for $30. At 2:00 PM I get stuck on the bus at the Inner harbor. I have to pick up Garren from school at 2:30 PM, so I talk a Ukrainian cabby into giving me a lift. I had also bought a rattan stick for Garren, and present it to him on the way home. We have an interesting conversation on the way home:

"Daddy, do I fight the bad boys with this?"

"No, that stick is for when you take walks with mom, for dogs and rats and such."

"But what about the bad boys, will they be back?"

"Yes, they'll be back."

"Do I arrest them?"

"No. Your job is to look out for the enemy, warn me, and then call nine-one-one."

"Okay Daddy."

4:00 p.m. Wednesday

No sign of the punks. Jerad is sitting on the porch with a friend and Garren is shooting cowboys and Indians with his newest dart gun. So I step into the shower. As soon as I get wet Garren opens the bathroom door, "They're back Daddy—big ones!"

I pull on my sweat pants, grab the 30-dollar stick and step outside to see Jerad and his friend frozen in fear on the front sidewalk. As I tie back my hair on the porch I notice Dave taking up a ringside seat across the street.

The fat white girl and the tall white boy were in the middle of the street in a support role [mouth].

The big black boy and a big white boy were in the parking lane, armed with bottles, in a backup role [meat]. In the gutter were two large black men in their mid-twenties. One had a bottle, the other a brick.

The one with the brick had a scar across his face, he looked at Jerad [5, 6" 120 lbs, and had never been in a fight in his life] and said, "Are you the one we're sposed ta do?"

I'm not going to lose this. Not a chance. I turn to Garren, "Call nine-one-one from upstairs in case they get through!"

It only takes me three strides to clear all 18 steps to my bedroom. I grab my shotgun [an old breach-loader] and two shells, and run back downstairs. I move so fast that Scar has only taken two steps toward Jerad by the time I am back on the porch slamming the breech shut. I am no longer thinking, just acting. I become irate with the fact that they only take one step back when I load the weapon. June, the nice black lady that lives next door, is bringing her groceries in. She is five feet from me, and kind of shocked.

I yell, "How many of you niggers wanna die today?"

June answers, "Not me!" and darts inside with her groceries.

The big black boy speaks, "You gotta worry. We know where you live. We'll burn your house down."

I feel myself getting closer to the men. The butt of the shotgun is pressed tightly against my shoulder. I can't hear the hammer cock back, but I can hear some maniac screaming about hunting and eating people, raping their mothers and sisters, barbequing their dogs and drinking their blood. Scar and his partner are not backing up fast enough and all I can think about is blowing an entire head off of a body at close range before beating every other living thing in the street to death with the big piece of oak and steel in my hands. They still aren't backing up fast enough! A big booming voice cuts through the insane stream of threats that is pouring out of me. It is Dave's voice and it says, "Don't do it Jim!"

With that the enemy breaks and runs, with me chasing them, telling them what bus stop I use at what times and swearing to exterminate their entire neighborhood...

Dave yells, "You idiot, put the gun away!"

I listen to him. When I make it up to the bedroom Garren is still on the phone with the moronic 911 operator, "My daddy is fighting bad boys in the yard. I told you the address already! No, I can't spell it. I'm only five-years-old!"

He slams the phone down, "Daddy, I think they're coming. But they're not too smart. I think they'll get lost."

Forty minutes later, after Dave has chewed me out, and Jerad's friends have come to view me as if I am some museum exhibit of early man, a fat, short, pasty-faced cop shows up and questions Jerad and me about our criminal history. He runs checks on us, and is not the least bit concerned about any description of the people that had come to my house, to beat my son to death, because he did not agree to be robbed outside of the liquor store.

Monday, 2:00 p.m., Belair-Edison, the neighborhood of my enemies

I am surrounded by over 200 high-school age students, winos, and assorted criminals as I walk from Erdman Avenue up Belair Road to the #15 Bus stop in front of Miss Lilly's convenience store. I get worried when I realize that I would only be able to recognize Scar. I check both my razors and my screw-driver, figuring on taking a couple with me. After all I had told them where and when to find me. I get on the back of the bus and stand in the aisle. I hear someone whisper something about a "big gun".

I never saw or recognized Scar or any of the others again.

I was hunted through this neighborhood on two other occasions. Once I managed to arm myself at a local liquor store with a 20-ounce long neck, and was followed no further by the two who stalked me and waited for me to emerge from the liquor store.

The other time, again followed by two young men, I turned left into Herring Run Park just before Parkside Drive [where my cousin Suzy was mugged]. When they followed me I quickened my pace until I was under the trees and could not be seen by any passing police cruiser; the police being the protectors of those who so often hunted me. When the two boys rounded the bend I drew my Othello and waived them forward. They turned and ran, and I took a nice walk in the park. At this age, I was still young enough to enjoy being hunted. In fact, I stopped long enough to strip a sapling and fashion a spear out of it, which I did cache in the Y of a large tree behind the old pumping station. I wonder if my spear is still there?

Did that last paragraph disturb you? Imagine how I felt last night when I found this in the middle of my 11-year-old rough draft. By age 33, 15 years of living in Baltimore City had resulted in me reverting to total barbarism. I had devolved almost completely.

Chapter 4

Outmanned

> *"I* am the mightiest! *I* am the man..."
> *-The Epic of Gilgamesh*

What follows are some poignant tales of predation; classic predation by men upon the weak. I really felt for these people when I interviewed them. I can offer little advice for people like them. I simply include their stories here so that they may at least have the last word concerning their terrible experiences.

Janice
#19-13: night, seconds, first-person defender

"I was eighteen, getting off work at about One in the morning, taking the bus home from downtown. I was sitting right in front of the back door on the bus, and these two black boys started talking to me. I was trying to avoid them. I said just enough to get by so that they wouldn't think I was prejudiced. They asked for cigarettes and I gave them each one. They could tell I was trying to avoid them. They were testing me, and didn't bother me anymore for a while.

They lit up, so I lit one. The bus driver—a big heavy black chick—didn't say anything to them, but made me put mine out. That made me a little angry.

When their stop came the one smacked me across the face as they got off. That really bothered me. I haven't taken the bus since. It's not safe for a white woman. If the car's not working I hire a cab or call out."

Janice was a coworker—a doughnut maker. Her icing used to come in mixed with my ice cream. Shortly after this interview she lost her car. Shortly after that she ran out of cab money. Shortly after that she approached me, "I have to take the bus or I'm going to lose my job, can you go with me?"

I wasn't thrilled with this. Female companions attract scum. Eight hours later we're at a bus stop in the howling February cold uptown, and I'm threatening to maim a panhandler who won't leave this chick alone. A half-hour later we are on the bus behind a man so massive that his seat is so stressed he's virtually in our lap, and baby cockroaches are crawling from his nappy lint covered hair, across his neck rolls and under his shirt-collar. She shakes in disgust.

A half-hour after that we are standing at an abandoned transfer point waiting for a bus that is 20-minutes late in sub-zero wind-chill. As she stands before me crying, teeth-chattering, and rubbing the arms of her inadequate pink jacket, she asks if she can huddle up inside of my trench coat.

When she finally stops shaking she puts her hands on my hips and looks up into my eyes, "You've been doing this for fifteen years? God, your life sucks. I would rather die than live like this. If I don't have wheels by Monday I'm killing myself!"

Red Boot Lady
#58-14: day, seconds, first-person defender

"I was a small boy; very small—frail even. I was thirteen. I had the best art picture in class, and this girl was jealous, so she grabbed it and tore it up. When I reached for it she pulled a can of silly-string from her pants pocket and sprayed me. I was trying to take the can from her. We were wrestling for it.

Mister Smith—a big black teacher, a body-builder—came up and spun me around by the shoulder and punched me in the stomach. The pain was terrible. I was on the floor and doubled-up. Everybody thought I was foolin'. Mister Smith said, 'He ain't hurt.'

This lady teacher—none of us liked—came up and said, 'Call the ambulance or I'm calling the police.'

We never liked that teacher—reading all the time, wore red boots. But the ambulance driver said I would have died. After her (looks to heaven) saving my life I never had a bad word to say about her.

My intestines had burst. (Pulls up shirt to expose jagged scar) It took thirty-two stitches just to close it. They could see the imprint of his ring on the X-ray. I suffer terrible bouts of pain to this day. It kept me out of the military, the way they had to patch up my insides. Couldn't never play sports. Sometimes I jus' double-over in knots.

When I woke up in the hospital bed mister Smith was right there besides me, in his own bed! True story. No foolin'. My oldest brother—who was an adult, my brothers being much older than me— beat him up. Beat him real bad. Then he left town to avoid trouble from the law. My mother didn't press charges 'cause of that. I want you to use his real name so that people will know what kind of man he was—a big muscular man beatin' on a little boy. It shouldn't be that way. He should have at least got in trouble.

Mister Smith got transferred to another school, but didn't lose his job. I always wanted to sue him. But by the time I looked into it the lawyers said that it had been too long. It was a terrible event, and still gives me pain to this day. But I'm alive, thanks to that lady teacher with the red boots that nobody liked. I like her now."

-Little Mike

Puppet
#46—08: night, minutes, first-person defender
"I had to be twenty-one. It was about Seventy-six—summertime. I worked at a fancy book store. I was five feet tall and weighed ninety pounds. I never was big. I had a friend that was big. She could fight most men. But even she was beaten

by her husband. He used to ruin all of her pretty things too. Every time he threw her out all her home interiors would be destroyed when she came back.

We were separated—my Ex and me. He was with his friends. I was with mine. We both ended up at the same bar with our friends. He asked me something. I don't know what I said, but the next thing I knew he was dragging me up the street on my back. That's a long fucking street, especially when you are being dragged on your back by your hair. This carload of guys rode by with drinks in their hands and said, 'Yeah, kill the bitch!'

Men are such fucking pigs. I was screaming. My back was raw, especially the shoulder blades—painful. Most men will not lift a finger to help you. They're pigs, fucking pigs! They are probably out there doing the same thing to their women. The ones who won't help—which is most of them around here (old South Baltimore)—are the ones that are doing the same thing to their women, and they wouldn't want anybody butting in when they're beating their women up.

That was a terrible situation to be in. I couldn't get up. I was on my back, held by the hair, and couldn't get up. I was being dragged like a cave woman. I felt like a cave woman. The next day when I got to work I really hurt. My back was bleeding all day long."

Pepper
#07-25: day, hours, first-person defender

"When I first met Cray, around Nineteen-eighty, I was separated from my husband. My husband and his brother were friends. He walked to the liquor store with me one night and we just started talking—that was it. He was little, about five-six, built little. He had frizzy brown hair and his teeth weren't real straight. He wasn't as ugly as his brother—he was real ugly. He wasn't good looking. His teeth probably ruined him. I guess I was lonely. He was somebody to talk to, and he didn't have many friends, so he devoted more of his time to me. He paid attention to me.

He was in and out of jail since about nine; lived with his mother and sometimes his brothers. His real ugly brother threw him out for dating me, and he moved in with this girl that his not-so-ugly brother dated once-in-a-while. She had five kids and was a mess. It was Historic Dundalk, in a row home.

Photo #4: The neighborhood where Pepper used to visit Cray at the time of the attack.

I went out with him for a month—visited him there a couple of times. He had a hard time having sex. He was used to men having sex with him in prison and had a hard time getting it hard. I got involved with him and didn't want to hurt his feelings. He was younger than me by two years—maybe eighteen. I didn't want to continue seeing him but didn't know how to tell him.

I was supposed to be at a baby shower at Seven-p.m. Friday—a stupid time to have a baby shower, but that's when these people had it. Me and Mary, the girl he was living with, had been out with these two guys on Thursday night. He kept questioning her about it, and I don't know what she told him.

He called me at around Twelve-p.m. Friday, and asked me to come over so we could talk. I got dressed and headed over there around One O'clock. When I went in the house Mary was sitting around with her kids, two of whom were teenage boys, and a man. She told me he was down the basement—that's where he slept. So I went down and he was very drunk and started asking me questions about where I was—like it was any of his business anyway.

I lied. I don't remember what I told him. Of course I don't know what she told him. Then he started going crazy, holding me with one hand and punching me with the other. I became dizzy and a long time seemed to pass while I was screaming. I was screaming for Mary to call the police. But she wouldn't because she had trouble with her kids stealing and selling drugs and didn't want the police in the house.

I tried to get up the stairs—many times—and he would pull me back down. I couldn't get away and thought he'd really kill me. He made me give him a blow job. He couldn't cum. Every time I'd stop he'd bang my head into the concrete floor. He was drinking moonshine the whole time. I should have bit it off. That's how it should have ended. I don't know if it occurred to me then—it would now!

When You're Food

He choked me on the bed, and choked me standing up against the wall, and was constantly banging my head off the wall. I couldn't breathe and it hurt. The walls were cement, and it felt like my head was going to bust open. I heard the sound of my head hitting the wall—it was loud, and there was a whole house full of people. He kept saying, 'Where was you at bitch?' with that black accent from prison.

Every time I would answer he would say, 'You lyin' bitch. Now tell me where you was at!', and he'd smack me.

He told me, 'Let's go. You're takin' me for a ride.'

I grabbed my purse and he walked me out the basement door. He was right there next to me, and I thought he was going to kill me. I thought of running, and how I was going to get out of this. Running was a problem. He was real fast, and there was no place to hide. Then he said, 'Don't even think about it.'

He made me let him in first. I got in, started it up, and asked him where he was going. He said, 'Jus' drive bitch.'

While I was driving he kept questioning, choking and slapping me. I was getting pretty hysterical by then."

Interlude: Are you judging this woman harshly for being a complaisant victim? I don't know if you were keeping count. But I was, and during the course of the initial assault in the basement, which appears to *have lasted for about an hour, Pepper suffered at least 3 concussions, with two of these being countercoup or "double" concussions. At this point, most professional boxers are no longer able to think, and fight on instinct only. I once received a severe concussion at the start of a stick fight, and remember nothing about the fight other than the referee raising my hand when it was over. I have fought through 10 concussions, but **never** intelligently: snarling, spewed blood, staggering toward my opponents until they lost heart and quit or the ref stopped it. If she was a quarterback she would have been taken off the field and put in an ambulance. So, keep in mind, that Pepper would have been acting on **her** instincts once her brain was sloshed around within her little skull and bruised the first few times.*

"We were riding down Eastern Avenue right by the police station. I was going to stop and run in, and he said, 'Don't even think about it. I have a knife in my pocket.'

He had his hand in his jacket pocket while he said it. He slapped me a couple of times and I kept on driving. I was a mess by then. He still had this bottle of moonshine and continued to drink. We pulled up to a stop light, and a cab stopped on my side. So I said, 'Please, help me, call the police for me.'

The cabby was an older man. He looked over and was smiling, held his can of beer up to Cray, and toasted him. Cray then toasted him with his bottle of moonshine. Then he said, 'Go bitch.'

When You're Food

We drove around for a while longer and he choked and punched me for a while. Then he said, 'Go back home bitch.'

Back into the basement again. The same thing all over again: slapping; questioning; choking; punching; head-smashing. I was too tired to scream anymore. I passed out a few times. I would come too while he was slapping me. I think that's why he slapped me, to wake me back up so I would know it while he beat on me. Eventually he got really drunk, and I talked him into letting me return my sister's car. I was never so relieved in my life!

When I went upstairs Mary looked at my lumpy head and smashed face and said, 'I'm so sorry. I didn't realize he was doing all that to you.'

I said, 'Don't you ever talk to me again.'

There was plenty of people up there, even a guy.

I drove off, stopped at the Drug City [she was functioning according to **her** instincts], bought a couple of sleepers for the baby, and drove to my mother's house. I guess that all took about twenty minutes. It was about five when I got to Mom's. I guess the beating lasted from one-fifteen to four-thirty.

My mother and sister were home and Cray was on the phone trying to apologize. I hung up on him. My mother said, 'What-the-Hell happened to you?'

They took me to the hospital. I had a bad concussion, cut lips, black-eyes, broken nose, swollen face, and really big knots on the back of my head. They gave me pain pills and told me not to go to sleep for a couple of hours.

My sister took me to the police station. The cops asked me what happened, who did it, and got a warrant out for him. Nothing happened legally. After they arrested him they let him out and he stalked me every day—hid behind the bushes at the bus stop. So I borrowed my sister's car and drove instead.

When I went to court he was in jail for robbery. The judge said that he was facing enough time, that I didn't have to press charges, and that he would leave it in 'stet', so if he got out and bothered me I could open the case back up. I was mad. I wanted him to do time—forever. He got nothing— no time for what he did to me.

While he was in prison he wrote me a letter. That's the last I heard of him. I found out he had naked pictures of me—he used to sneak in and snap pictures when I was in the shower—and was showing them to guys in prison. A friend of mine was dating a murderer—she eventually married him—a big guy, a real nice guy. Don't know why he killed the person. He took the pictures from Cray in prison and sent them to my girlfriend so that she could destroy them."

As I penned this last line, Pepper [a 100-pound bar maid] reached across the bar and ran her palm over my enlarged punching knuckles, "Those are sharp ones, the kind that hurt."

She said it as a matter-of-factly as some old gym rat, and it sent a chill up my spine.

Chapter 5

Outgunned

Some facts about gun violence:

-45% of gunmen are acting as part of a violent group, usually with a single accomplice.

-89% of gunmen target lone individuals.

-88% of gun violence occurs outside.

-50% of gun violence consists of armed robberies.

-25% of gun violence consists of assaults, including murders.

-25% of gun violence consists of police usage and self-defense [often illegal].

Photo #5: The most violent area in Northeast Baltimore, a quarter-mile from the Eastern District Court House, which overlooks a regular dog-fighting venue.

Photos #6 & #7: The mouths of two alleys in Northeast Baltimore where handgun robberies have occurred. Both crimes involved a victim that was using the bisecting sidewalk of the alley from which the gunman emerged, each time with an unarmed accomplice.

The first few anecdotes will consist of typical accounts, followed by some more engrossing tales.

Ron Spade
#58-01: night, seconds, first-person defender

"This was in Nineteen-eighty, on a Saturday night, in East Baltimore. I was managing the gas station at Orleans and Washington. I was on the phone and two guys walked up to the booth. Was before the bullet-proof glass. I turn around and look and he's standing there with a twenty-two revolver, 'Ain't no sense gettin' hurt ova a white-man's money. Jus' give it to me.'

Management always told us, 'Don't worry about the money. Worry about yourself.'

I had just made a deposit. So I gave them the fifty bucks and they took off running."

Brett
#57-23: day, seconds, first-person defender

"It was a cold night. I was walking home from a friend's—about Eleven or Twelve at night— through the alley behind my apartment. This guy was walking toward me. At about four or five feet away he demanded money. I said I didn't have any and he produced a firearm—a shiny nine-millimeter in my face. He was right on me. I started using the word sir a lot, showed him my wallet was empty, turned my pockets inside out, and asked him if I could keep my I.D. He gave me a funny look and that's when I closed my eyes. He said, 'You motherfucker, don't ever let me see you back here again.'

He started to back away and I hurried off."

Tommy
#49-09: night, seconds, first-person aggressor

"Was hangin' wit da boyz on da corna. Old dude yells from his porch fo us to quiet down. A friend—not a very cool friend—was holdin' my thirty-eight and he flashed it. The old dude went inside en my boy's laughin'. Then the old dude pop back out wit' the biggest handgun I eva saw, Boom! One shot en we was off. Anotha friend take it in da arm; lost fifty percent of 'is tricep muscle. Lucky it didn't hit da bone."

Spin

Spin was a drug trafficker who moved dope from the Northeast through South Baltimore, to Cherry Hill, a notorious suburb. I often sat behind him, sometimes taking notes, as he held court with his hangers-on at the back of the #19 Bus. The following tales concern two associates of his. Depending on your politics he is either the Bill Clinton or William F. Buckley of crack dealers. He always referred to himself as "Yo Smart Nigga."

Krazee

"Yo, yo Krazee Nigga be too dependable! We jus' profilin', lookin' fo a bitch o' two. Yo Easy Nigga drivin', yo Krazee Nigga lookin' cruel, en yo Smart Nigga stylin'. We goin' through a light en see yo

Cheap-dealin' Nigga on da corna. Yo Krazee Nigga kick open da passanga side doe—while Easy still drivin'! Step to da curb, slap, bank, en kick the nigga—lookout, out come da nine!—and cap his Cheap-dealin' ass! He ged back in hardly befoe we stop. He all quiet, eatin' a Snickas, en Yo Smart Nigga be, 'Yeah, it's all good', 'cause Yo Smart Nigga gots ta have his Krazee Nigga."

Stupit

"Yo, how 'bout yo Stupit Nigga tryin' ta bank a Secret Service agent!?! How stupit can one nigga be? (Laughter) Think he gots hiself a Jew, but gots one a Clinton's crew! (Hysterical spit-producing laughter) This nigga dumba den yo Dumb Nigga.— least ways he got shot by a regala cop who can be sued. Who dis stupit nigga gonna sue? Think DaNiro bad? Shiiit, Clinton got da crew: merciless white-boys; killa spy bitchez, smart-fucking Jews, and prayin' niggas too!"

Weston
14-08: day, seconds, first-person-defender

Weston hung up the phone outside of a convenience store , turned around, and had the barrel of a 3.57 pressed against his nose by an older man, who demanded all 40 of his twenty-dollar bills...

"...He also took my gold comb pendant, worth seven-hundred dollars. That was a nice comb. I ran into the guy not long ago. He was panhandlin'. Didn't even recognize me—asked me for a handout.

I wanted to hurt him bad. But I've given up that street life, and I had my wife with me."

Gus

"This was the Thursday before Christmas back in the early nineties. I was at home in my second-story apartment. I didn't have negative on my mind; wasn't expectin' trouble. I heard a knock on the door and saw this UPS driver. When I opened the door he threw a gun up under my cheek; a nine. He said, 'Don't say nothin'.'

A guy with a big long Rambo knife come in behine. They was big bruthas, two bruthas from Temple Hill Maryland, six-four, nice size guys. This was a complicated case. These guys were wanted over in Prince George's County four rapin' and robbin' two women. They were very dangerous.

The brutha with the gun did all the talkin'. I reckon he thought I was a dealer. They must a thought my house was a drug house. He said, 'Anybody in the house?'

I said, 'No', and he pushed me into the back bedroom while the guy with the knife searched the house. He came back into the bedroom—had cut the cord off the iron—and tied me up on the floor like I was a cow rustled to the ground, face down on the floor like a hog.

The dude sat on my bed and loaded up his gun—I didn't know it was unloaded—and said, 'We're gonna kill ya.'

The dude told me that! He said, 'Where the money at?'

The other guy was robbin' the house, and called him in the other room and said he needed help tryin' ta get the TV out. You know how they say the Lord be by your side? I got untied. I jumped out the second-floor window. I landed on my knee. At the present time there was no thinkin' 'bout no pain. The guy shot out the window at me twice, missing into the ground. They ran out the front door after me. But trust me, when you scared, you gone!

I made it up the rental office, and had them call the police. They got into their car and got caught by the Park Police for speeding. They didn't get no time for mine. They got to let somethin' go so they can plea-bargain. They got twenty years, but not on mine, which I thought was messed up."

Sleepy
#56-08: night, seconds, first-person defender
"This was in Cherry Hill at the end of summer. Was a accident really. These two guys walked up, one had a thirty-eight, the otha a nine. They were afta someone else and I jus' happened to be there conversatin' with this guy. He was selling drugs for them and was messin' with their money.

When they came up we bolted, and they started shootin'. My friend got hit with two nine millimeters in the spine, and was paralyzed. By me runin' I got shot in the back with one thirty-eight slug, and the otha hit me in the buttocks, came out, grazed ma groans, and hit me in the leg, where it got lodged behine the bone. I walked—in shock—to my mother's house, and was taken to the hospital.

It was not as bad as being stabbed—you're more in shock after being shot and can appreciate it less. However, I was worried about being able to have sex after that. But the nurse that attended me, we ended up havin' a chyle together. So somethin' positive did come of it.

There was no arrests or anything. It's a low-income area. The cops think, 'Shoot, its one less for us to worry with.' That's the cops attitude in low-income areas. Can't say I blame 'um."

S. J.

"This was April Second, Nineteen-seventy-two, Easter Sunday, around Nine PM. I was home studying—was in college at the time. I got a phone call from my sister's boyfriend. They were trying to get into the Latin Casino—a popular club at the time—and needed an I.D. and a ride home. I picked them up in a 1963 V.W. bus—I was a hippie (rolls eyes).

We bought about a dozen beers and went to their friend Mary's apartment. It was in an apartment complex at the corner of Bonsell and Boston—a basement apartment—in a working class neighborhood.

There was my sister, Randy, Mary, her little kids, and Nate—a black guy—a friend of Randy's. We were just sitting around drinking beer in the living room when there was a knock on the door. When Mary answered the door there were four guys at the door: a young kid who left right away; one nondescript guy; a big Italian monstrosity; and Richard Rositer, an ugly piece of white trash (tall, thin, redhead with pockmarked face). She thought they were our friends and we thought she knew them.

They were looking for a guy that wasn't there. Randy walked up to them and said, 'Hey man got any I.D.?'

Rositer said, 'Yeah, I got some I.D.', and backhanded Randy across the face with a pistol; a little twenty-two. There was a nick on his chin and my sister was tending to him. Nate tried to get into the kitchen to use the phone, and Rositer said, 'Sit down nigger.'

He sat down next to the front door. This guy Rositer was obviously the boss, and said, 'Go check the apartment.'

He was looking for a guy named Billy. Billy was the boyfriend of Randy's sister, who would babysit for Mary while Mary was working as a waitress. He suspected Billy of something. I was sitting there watching this shit; doing nothing, saying nothing. The two guys checked the apartment and said, 'He's not here.'

Randy walked out of the bathroom after being tended to. Rositer—he had put the gun back in his waistband—walked up to shake his hand and said, 'Hey man, sorry.'

Randy was like, 'Fuck you! I'll get you. I ain't shaking your hand.'

When You're Food

He's walking away while he's threatening Rositer, and the guy pulled his gun out, aimed, shot, and missed from ten feet. When he missed from that close I thought maybe he had blanks. A brew-ha breaks out: kids; women; people getting scared and making noise. And I'm sitting there drinking beer. I realized this was it. I was fine-tuned; one of those 'This is it!' situations.

They start to leave. The door is to the left. Nate is sitting to the right. When Rositer walks out—he's last—Nate gets up and kicks the guy. In retrospect I must admit that I was with some really stupid people. Rositer turns around and shoots Nate in the shoulder. He falls down and the other two guys come in and start beating the fuck out of him, punching him while he's on the floor.

Remember, it was Nineteen-seventy-two. Black men were heroes. I felt like I had to do something, all hundred-and-fifty pounds of me. I tried to pull off the big Italian guy, and he spins around, grabs me, and was ready to smash me with a punch, when Rositer came up, put the gun to my left side—not actually pressing it against me—and shot me.

I'm on the floor in agony. They were all tending to Nate, and were saying to me, 'What-the-Hell is the matter with you?'

They got me up on the couch. When the cops got there I heard the cop on the radio say, 'We've got one shot in the shoulder, and'...he comes over to me and touches where the bullet is lodged under the skin (on the right side)...'and let me see, down here, one in the side.'

I was conscious up into the operating room—tubes all in me. I just remember thinking that James Arness on Gun Smoke survived a lot more than this. That was a very strange out-of-body experience, and it helped me mentally. I was singing—in my brain—the song Horse with No Name by America. They asked me if I had any drug experience. I said, 'Yeah.', and it almost came back to haunt me.

The bullet—it was only a twenty-two thank God—went in the left side, through the stomach, the colon, the liver, and shattered the spleen. Eventually this will kill me—that ugly fuck Rositer will kill me! Because the spleen is part of the immune system I am susceptible to pneumonic viruses, and have to get inoculated every six years.

I was in the hospital for thirteen days. Nate never did come to visit. They had to pump my stomach continuously. I was so thirsty! This older guy who shared the room with me would put some ice in my mouth to give me some relief. After eight days I finally got to take a shit. What a relief!

This happened during my mid-terms. I would have continued with school. But it was too much. I became a construction worker. Perhaps I'm lucky that I didn't continue with school. I majored in accounting. Most of the guys I went to school with ended up working for the IRS. Could you imagine working for that monstrous fucking bureaucracy? What a miserable existence that must be.

When You're Food

A lot of my friends went to Nam and got shot. I didn't dodge the draft or get a deferment. But I kind'a felt like I was a coward. That experience let me know I wasn't. The best part about it was that I finally got a call to I.D. Richard Rositer. I went to court, and they told me to point him out. They hadn't arrested him for the shooting. He was picked up for something else. He had shaved and cut-and-dyed his hair. But he still had the pockmarks on his face. When we went to trial the prosecutor said that he agreed to plead guilty to two counts of assault, and that he could walk in a jury trial. The judge was black. We told our story. The judge gave him eight years. He appealed it. He brought a character witness. But the judge that heard the appeal said that he ought to be glad it wasn't his case, because he would have given him thirty years."

Chapter 6

Outnumbered

The mass attack is the big dog of predatory violence, with 29% of all violence being initiated by a group. Below I have divided mass aggressions into 4 categories, and have provided statistics concerning the salient points of survival. All violence is defined as the 1675 acts of violence I collected in interviews from 1996 to 2000. Of these, 482 acts of violence qualify as mass aggressions. I have included a column for all violence (first column) as a base-line, and one for those individual aggressors who have attacked groups (last column), as an indication of how much just being the aggressor effects a combatant's chances of success.

Context & Results

All V.	2-on-1	3-on-1	4-on-1	Group-on-group	Individual-on-group*
% of defender successes**					
13%	10%	12%	12%	9%	21%
% of aggressor successes					
57%	70%	73%	75%	82%	55%
%of defenders injured***					
36%	48%	49%	58%	60%	33%
%of aggressors injured					
9%	7%	11%	9%	12%	11%
% of defender deaths					
4%	5%	9%	6%	14%	8%
% of aggressor deaths					
1%	1%	1%	1%	0%	3%
% of defender legalities****					
7 %	3%	8%	13%	6%	3%
% of aggressor legalities					
13%	16%	11%	15%	19%	24%

*%4 of all violence is initiated by an individual against a group
**imposed will on adversary

Note: only 70% of violence was decisive, with 30% being unresolved. So the aggressors and defenders in this study are literally left to fight over %70 of the violence pie.

***required medical attention
****arrest, citation, civil or legal charges

4-on-1 context

The average size of attacking groups was 6. That is only based on verifiable accounts though. Keep in mind that, once a group of attackers exceeds three, it becomes very difficult for most defenders to provide an accurate after-action count.

Group-on-group context

Defender group sizes: 2=68%; 3=9%; 4+=23%

Aggressor group size: 2=45%; 3=14%; 4=41%

For some reason, groups of 3 are unlikely to be involved as aggressors or targeted as defenders.

Impressions

The most surprising aspect was that a lone defender has just about the same odds of success against an individual, a pair, a trio, or a pack. Also note the increased violence of 3-on-1s and group-on-groups over 2-on-1s and 4-on-1s. The most lethal attacks are those, by a group targeting a group. The findings here support aggression as the primary indicator of success, with numbers secondary.

Tarzan the Anorexic, an avoidance case-study

A Saturday in July, 1994, 12:30 p.m., the Belair-Edison Neighborhood in Northeast Baltimore

I had been out to work since 8:00 p.m. Friday. I am busing it home because the new truck I had just purchased for my wife had been vandalized by an unsuccessful auto-thief around midnight. I am feeling abrasive. I step off the #22 Bus at Erdman and Belair, and walk past an occupied doorway. From the mouth of this concrete cave a large bum emerges, "Yo, give me money!"

I switch my handbag to my left hand, put my right palm on the butt of the utility knife behind my belt buckle, and step up into his face snarling, "I've got six-hundred-and-seventeen dollars in my pocket. If you can take it it's yours."

He backs off, "Yo Tarzan, I'm jus' aksin. If you wanna fight fo yo money tell dem tree on da corna what chew got."

He indicates three young thugs looking our way. If I avoid them they will hunt me. If I confront them they will fight me. I must walk close by them without antagonizing them or showing fear. They are turning their attention to a gorgeous 6-foot-eight-inches-in-heels, 200 pound black woman. She is dressed in a tight red miniskirt and red-lace halter-top, and is blatantly ignoring them as she window shops. She is my out. I will play sexist barbarian at her expense. Yes, Tarzan will put his case of jungle fever on display and slide by like he is just another brutha...

I fix the ebony Amazon with a penetrating leer, as if I am a scout for King Magazine. I walk past the thugs, turning my head as I admire her long legs. The thugs are checking her out too. She is between us as they lean against the wall—their leader sucking on a lollypop—and I pass on the street-side. She stops, looks down at me over her broad left shoulder, bats her inch-long eye-lashes, and smiles, "Hey baby, if you like it that much you can have my number."

I hear the lollypop smack on the pavement as I choke on my inadequate reply, and then scurry off like a roach suddenly caught under the glare of the kitchen light.

I don't know her name, but she got me by those three, emasculating all four of us with one sentence.

Suffice it to say that all such situations are bad-odds encounters and should be avoided. What follows are tales of group aggressions that were not avoided. These will be presented below in the order used in the table above: 2-on-1s, 3-on-1s, 4+-on-1s and group-on-group.

2-on-1s

Getting Burned
57-07: night, seconds, eye-witness

Gumby was a chubby wannabe skinhead sporting racist and obscene tattoos and a menacing go-tee. Last night he had ripped off two black crack dealers on this very ball court. On this night he just came to play ball. The two dealers rushed him at the foul line and knocked him to the ground. As he was getting to his feet the smaller dealer doused him on the left side from face to fingers with lighter fluid. The other dealer touched a lighter to Gumby, who became an example to all.

3-on-1s

I ain't No White-boy!
#42-19: day, seconds, first-person defender

Haynes (a stocky middle-aged former boxer) was waiting for the #1 Bus when three boys approached him. The medium-sized leader of the group said, "Hey old man, give us yo money!"

"Shit, I ain't no white-boy! Who-da-Hell dey think I am! Ha? Shiiit, I go ta war ova what I work for! They was kids so I didn't knife 'em—showed restraint. I broke his nose with a jab and palmed his solar-plexus ta stop 'im. I then grab the little one en drag his ass around while I chase the big one. Cops arrested me, despite the witnesses who said I was in the right. Cops are worthless. Judge threw it out."

Suzy
#28-09: night, seconds, first-person defender
"I was riding my bike from Fells Point to Federal Hill with dirty laundry in my backpack. They must of thought I had something good in there. But it was just dirty undies—must a smelled good. I was riding on the sidewalk by the water in between the World Trade Center and the Aquarium. It was about Eight on a Friday night; summertime. It was pretty busy. Must have been ten people watching, including some healthy men.

I think I got knocked out. I was out of it— getting the shit beat out of me, laying on my left side. Some of them were pulling on my backpack, bouncing me up-and-down. Somebody else was pulling on my bike. My left leg was caught up in the bike, between the top and the middle bars, and they kept on pulling, tearing my ligaments. I wasn't feeling anything. Something triggered them, and they ran away—a mixed race group of teen-agers; three, maybe four of them. There was a broomstick broken between the spokes of my front wheel. They obviously saw me coming.

I had to remove the stick, and I peddled the bike one-footed about two miles to my brother's house. I got to my brother's and he kept bugging me to go to the hospital, and I was like, 'No.'

The next morning I woke and it hurt so bad I could hardly breathe. I lived on the third floor and hobbled over to my neighbor's to get a ride to the hospital. The doctor said, 'We're just going to drain some of this fluid from your knee', and she sticks this huge needle in my knee and drains out this blood. She said that I had my ligaments torn, and put me in a cast.

I was working as a cook at the time, and had to ride the bus through the projects on my way to work. It took months to heal. The Metro system is a joke. I lived in D.C. and I was used to busses that got you someplace. The Baltimore Metro doesn't get you anywhere you want to go. Then—if you actually take the subway—you get to walk down this quarter-mile empty hallway with no security. Oh yeah, thanks! Just put me in the most vulnerable position imaginable!"

Author's note: All Baltimore area bus-lines are intentionally routed through the worst areas possible so that the needful classes have easy access to mass transit. This has the added benefit of bringing vulnerable prey into their hunting grounds as well.

Mary Ann
#36-11; day, seconds, eye-witness

"I was delivering auto-parts and I stopped by to say 'hi' to my brother Tommy. Tommy is such a nice guy—but he's so strong. He's six-one, two-seventy-five. I once saw him carry a five-hundred-pound iron wood-stove up our mother's front stairs and down into the basement.

When I stop by he comes out and notices these three big dudes sitting on the rear bumper of his pickup, and he's like 'What the fuck guys?' So they rush him, all big dudes—his size. He grabs one and slams him to the pavement—done! Grabs this other dude and throws him over the fucking bed out into the street—crunch! I'm like, 'Woah, what a fuckin' toss!'

Well, the other dude is like, 'I'm fucked', en just kind of stands there—frozen in fear—and lets Tommy grab him, 'Whip, toss, crunch'—another one clear over the truck and into the street! I'm like, 'Bro, I'm not sittin' on yer truck, okay!'

So the pigs roll up en me—sweet little me—explains how Tommy was attacked, and they just call the paramedics to scrape these fuckers up! 'Nice Bro.' He really is a nice, nice guy. You've gotta wonder why some idiots would bum-rush a dude that carries a hundred pound tool box in one hand and a generator under the other arm when he heads out to work in the morning."

Yeah, I know. I also want to get up tomorrow morning and see Tommy looking back at me in the mirror. They can't take our dreams away.

4+-on-1s

Duz
#59-02 and #12-02: night, minutes, first-person

To put this story in context, keep in mind that Duz, a former sparring partner of mine, is a freakishly strong person, a little Tommy. His head was so damned hard I used to pray that he would duck, because my hands would hurt so badly from punching him. I think his skull is actually a sculpted cinder block.

"I was sixteen. It was New Year's Eve, real cold out. There was like four of us and we went over this other guy's house in Rosedale for a party. There was probably ten or twelve other guys there that I didn't know—thought the other guys I was with knew. I was five-ten, maybe one-seventy. We was having a good time for maybe an hour. Mike comes up to me and says, 'The Fitch brothers want to fuck me up.' They didn't like him because of this girl. 'If any shit happens I want you to back me up.'

I said, 'Yeah.'

I didn't think much of it. Maybe another hour went by. The one Fitch brother wants to change the tunes and Mike says, 'Nah, leave it there, and I said, 'Yeah.'

Fitch says, 'Who are you? Why are you talking? Do you want to go out and fight about it?'

I said, 'Yeah.'

We went out in the guy's backyard. I remember the footing was really sloppy; like it had rained a lot and there was leaves all over the place. A couple of punches were thrown by both. Neither landed and we were down on the ground. When I went down I quickly had my arm around his neck and held him. I tried getting in the other arm but never did. It seemed like I had him in a choke forever. It was a long time. It went back and forth from a, 'this-mutherfucker's-going-to-die' choke to a 'kinda-got-a-choke' hold.

He almost got a reversal. I was still choking him and eventually got back on top, but at all times I was behind him. 'Ah yes', this was the most decisive choke of the night. Don't know if it was him being tired, or because it was a really good choke. He did say, 'Get the fuck off me. I can't breathe.'

I said, 'If I get up I'm getting my coat and glasses and leaving.' And the crowd that had gathered said, 'Yeah, just let 'im up man.'

Once it was a consensus opinion that I was going to leave, I let him up. We were out-numbered three-to-one. I let him up and walked inside down the basement. Mike was patting me on the back. I was pumped, but calm, cool and collective—as calm as you can be after choking some guy. Maybe I was naïve that way but I didn't see any danger coming.

All three of the Fitch brothers were six-one, six-two, built like baseball players. I got my coat half on, and as I was slipping my other arm into it, one of the Fitch brothers punched me in the face and knocked me into the stereo. The guy whose house it was said, 'We're going to fucking kill you now.'

The hit was on purpose. But I could have fallen anywhere. It was definitely the stereo that triggered the attack. I had my coat but not my glasses. I didn't get them back for months. They sure enough caught me by the time I got across the street. I was up against a car and they were punching and kicking. The furthest I went down was a crouch—that's when the kicks became more effective. Them boots—engineer boots were the style of the day—do a number on your face.

There was four, five, maybe six of them. I don't know. I didn't stop to count. I was worried about getting out of there. I heard Phoebus screaming for me to get-the-Hell out of there. Nobody helped. I remember that. It was kind'a like a crowd semi-circled in front. So I busted through like a football player and ran. They didn't chase. I ran down the street and caught up with Phoebus. My face was all messed up; both eyes black, nose bleeding, but no dental damage."

Duz is a supermarket manager, who was once run-over by two gunmen in a stolen car who tried and failed to rob him of the day's deposit. He did not miss our workout that night, and recalled, what to most would have been a horrifying event, as one of the most 'Fun' experiences of his life.

Ryk
#16-18: night, seconds, first-person defender

Ryk, a Ukrainian cabby, became lost in West Baltimore. While stopped at a traffic light with a car behind him, a group of perhaps 20 blacks formed a human chain to block his escape as two others approached his driver's-side and passenger-side doors. Ryk punched the accelerator, 'bumped over' a few bodies, and drove to a car wash in the County, where he washed the blood off of the car.

Vernon
#38-10: day, minutes, eye-witness

"I was sittin' in the school cafeteria when this boy filled his spoon with peas and made a little catapult out of it, sprayin' this one table with them mushy peas. The whole table; males, females, probably thirty kids, cleared and threw him down. They stood in a circle, hands on each other's shoulders to steady themselves, en jus stomped and kicked—so many that most had to crowd in and push through just to get in a lick. I finished my lunch en they was still kickin'. The teachers did nothin' to intervene. What was left wasn't movin' and didn't have no teeth in its head."

Baby Girl
#55-23: day, minutes, eye-witness

"This was on the Number Eight Line, southbound on Central. I was getting off school; coming from Dunbar High School. I'll never forget this. It was Three-o-Three p.m.. This was over a guy. The first girl was a tall brown-skinned female, kind'a pretty but tough. The other girl was a short dark-skinned attractive female; doin' the femininity thing—all into her womaness. She was also into the tall girl's guy.

The brown-skinned girl said—in class— something about staying away from her guy, and the dark-skinned girl mouths off about what he needs, and what she's got, you know...

Well, after school, the tall girl who's guy this really was, came outside taking off her shoes and putting on sneakers and greasing her face up with petroleum jelly. She was real serious. Her girls were with her too: five of them, six all together. Three had long hair and light skin, about one-forty-five each. And there were two thick girls: five-five, one-eighty and five-eight two-hundred.

They made sure she got on her bus first— they took a different bus—and stepped on. The dark-skinned girl was seated across from me in the back. The brown-skinned girl walked up to her and kicked her in the face—full extension. I was like 'Damn!' and she was bangin' her in her face. She had a good aim and didn't have ta hold her. She fell into the corner between the seats and they was holdin' the poles and stomping.

By this time I was up on my seat on my feet. The big girl jump-stomped her with two feet in the face! I was like, 'Oh my God!' Anybody and everybody was just kicking her!

Then the bus driver gets everybody off the bus and calls an ambulance. She—her face—was fucked up! Her head was busted—spent two months in shock trauma. When she came back to school it was her first and last day. The girls were going to get her again because they were suspended and wouldn't be able to cross the stage at graduation. She got a home tutor."

George
#50-09 & 10: day, minutes, first-person defender

"This was in 1958. I was fourteen, in seventh grade, walking home through Odonell Heights, toward Dundalk Avenue, between Odonell Street and the railroad tracks. We used to walk the train tracks home, take a short cut.

I hung in the school gangs. I joined because it was easier than getting beat up all the time, or paying protection dues. Whenever they would beat up somebody I would hang on the outside of the group—melted in to avoid the beating. I guess I was their psychological support.

The gang that got me was a different gang, a street gang, waiting by the railroad tracks like bandits, taking a toll so-to-speak. They stopped me and smacked me around a little. I had an uncle who was in the army and had fought in Europe that I confided in because my father was working all the time. He suggested that the next time I pick the biggest baddest one out and beat him up.

When You're Food

The leader of the gang was named Purdy, a community hoodlum; beat his mother up and broke into a cemetery building, sleeping in there, hiding from the police. He was big and husky and wore a denim jacket. The second time I walked home on the tracks it was fall—getting cold in the evening—they came down the hill hoopin' and hollerin'. I knew what was going to happen. I cut left downhill to go through the graveyard and they caught me on the path about a hundred feet from the tracks.

They surrounded me and Purdy ran his mouth. He was the leader and wanted money. I punched him in the face and his head didn't even move. It was like hitting a wall; didn't even phase him. That's when they started beating-the-Hell out of me.

I doubled up on the ground to try and protect myself from the hits and kicks, hiding my face. They went through my pockets, ripped my pants and belt off, put the belt around my neck and hog-tied me. They put the belt around your neck—it runs down your spine—and your pants are tying your hands to the belt, so when you struggle you choke yourself.

They left me on the ground and went up to the tracks and started throwing those big black porous railroad rocks. I couldn't see but could hear the whizzing, thumping, thudding sounds. I rolled on my side and pushed with my feet and shoulders, trying to use the shoulder like a hand to pull away, trying to get into the bushes for protection. They left me tied. The sun was going down and it was getting dark early. I was hog-tied under the bushes as it grew dark; struggling, choking, gasping.

Leroy Thompson had been punished and kept after school. He was the head of a gang from Odonell Heights. He was very powerful, like a little bull with a happy laugh. He was such a ruffian that I never ran with him. Leroy was the last one coming home from school that day, and he heard me, found me, and untied me. When I got home I was a mess. I told my mother I had been jumped, but not the extent."

Group-on-Group

Kenneth
#56-05: day, a minute, eye-witness

"I was coming down Eastern Avenue on the Twenty-three Line. It was packed; standing room only, all blacks, a black driver.

These two white-boys got on the bus. You had to stand in the aisle. They were juiced, had been drinkin'. The one says to his partner, 'Back in the day they would have gotten up and gone to the back so we could sit down.'

What a stupid thing to say. You can have your racism, but keep it to yourself, especially when you surrounded by a hundred niggas! His buddy hop off right then. They was all ova him—three men en two females—punching, kicking, stomping, beat him bad. I pleaded for him, 'Oh Lord, he didn't know what he said. He jus' a dumb white-boy. Let him be.'

Did no good. Othas sayin', 'Kill his fuckin' ass!'

I eventually got ta him and covered him with ma body—spread-eagle—until the next stop. As I pulled him off the bus they was still kickin' his ass. It was terrible but funny too.

He had all kinds a thanks for me. He had facial cuts and swelling so I called the paramedics from a pay phone."

Dan Funk

Dan is a bio-mechanical genius. He has played and coached multiple ball sports and combat sports and has very good mechanical recall. He's an easy interview.

#27-09 to #27-12: day, minutes, eye-witness

"It was the end of summer in Atlanta. It wasn't your conventional strip bar. It was a Ma and Pa place. You could get chips and stuff up front and go in the back and watch the girls dance for a three-dollar cover. The dancers were average girls from the area—girls you could talk to. This was just a topless friendly club—not totally nude—regular easy-going people. When you went in you never saw any bouncers.

We were there for about three hours—pretty looped up—when these three guys come in drunk, which isn't good. We noticed that John was walking to the bathroom and these guys were calling him names. One of the girls is sitting with one of these guys, and his pal is mad because she's sitting on his lap, 'That's my girl!' He stands up and punches at the guy but misses and hits the girl square in the face. She hits the ground and is up like a cat, ready to fight.

As she's getting up, from out of the back, the store, the kitchen and the DJ booth comes literally ten guys! Instant! Amazing! They converge on their table. As they are grabbing these guys she's trying to tear this guy's face off from behind and smashes a bottle over his head. One of the guys throws her off.

One guy punches him in the face, follows his punch and takes him to the floor, and has him mounted and is punching him while three other guys are stomping all the loose parts.

Another guy grabs his pal around the shoulders in a hug and drives him to the floor, and three to four guys are stomping, picking parts— they knew what they were doing—ankles, hands, anything that was out.

It seemed like an hour it was so scary. We thought it would break out among other patrons so we stood back and drank. We had time to finish a whole beer. This had to have been a ten minute beating. But we couldn't get another beer because everyone was involved; the dancer was back, the waitress and two barmaids are trying to get a piece!

They were covering in fetal positions after a while: stomps, kicks, grunts, screams, 'helps', cussin'. After about five more minutes of that some of the guys turned to hold off the girls—two had to hold the waitress down—and the others finished the official beating on these guys. You come in through the store, but you leave through a side entrance.

Someone had called the police. But the cops couldn't come in—don't know what was up with that. These two guys were semi-conscious. Two guys pick up one and swing him through the door—opening it with his head—out onto the lot, like yesterday's trash. The last guy lands on top of the first guy.

The police came over—didn't say a word—cuffed them, threw them into the back of the car, and drove off. An hour later the cops came back, sat down, had a beer, and enjoyed themselves.

That had to be the most brutal and efficient disposal of drunken idiots I've ever witnessed. It was just crazy, like the cooks, clerks, DJ, barmaids, waitress are all heat-seeking missiles armed and ready to launch. There wasn't really a bouncer per say in the place. The third guy just evaporated, disappeared when the attackers started coming out of the woodwork. Good instincts I'd say."

Little Mike & the B'mo Bammers
#58-06 to #58-13

"B'mo is DeeCee (Washington D.C.) for Baltimore. Bammers was an insult. It was another word for punk or chump. DeeCee used that name against Baltimore. There was about a hundred in our group on campus. There thirteen of us from Baltimore—the B'mo Bammers. There was DeeCee girls on campus and they liked some Baltimore guys so there was trouble.

We was pretty frightened, a long way from home, surrounded by DeeCee people. We used to sleep in the dorm. One guy got molested in there. Another guy had a fire-cracker set off in his ear and it brain-damaged him. One guy had his foot broken with a sledge hammer. We got to sleepin' with mop handles under our pillows in case they came. But they always got you one at a time.

There was a leader; one particular leader who instigated everything. We said, 'That's the one. Maybe if we get him that will put a pause to it.' When we saw this one guy from Baltimore, we thought they would leave us alone. I don't know his name. We called him Hercules. He was huge, real muscular.

In class everything was okay. But when you come outside the gangs are there, and you can't let them see the weakness in ya. We were outside smoking cigarettes. The gangs used to come into the campus through this hole in the fence, and there they were. This DeeCee guy came up to Hercules with a large military knife and tried to hit him with it like it was a stick. Hercules grabbed his wrist, then grabbed the knife. He held the knife up, looked at it, grabbed the blade, and bent it until it looked like a horseshoe, and threw it away. When them people saw that they left.

When we saw what he did we thought we were safe. But it must have done something to him mentally because he left the program. There had been thirteen of us that had come down on the bus. They kept getting us one at a time. They caught this one guy in the dorm and lit him up with lighter fluid.

I used to watch the basketball games. I couldn't play, but I liked to watch. This one DeeCee guy was real good, and I told him so, that he should be on a team. He said that he was too heavy and couldn't get on a team. He was an alright guy. I tried to encourage him to get on a team.

Eventually, they had gotten most of us. There was only two of us left: Big Tony and me. We were coming back from off-campus through the hole in the fence, and they were there: the leader and his one particular friend, his buddy.

His buddy run up besides me from behind and I felt this 'pow!' on my ear and seen this brick fall to the ground. I said, 'Ah, you hit me with a brick.'

That's when I saw this pipe. I tried to get to the leader but I got his buddy. There must have been lightnin' in that pipe. Because I broke his nose, his teeth, and messed up one of his eyes.

I had dropped the pipe and they were commin' from everywhere. Must have been hundreds of 'um; girls; gangs, people from off-campus. Tony and I looked at each other and we both said the same thing, 'We gonna die.'

Tony took out about five of 'em with a trash can. But they kept commin' and eventually beat us down. They beat me so bad I blacked out. When I woke up somebody was holding me like I was a baby. I heard a big voice say, 'Leave him alone.'

It was the basketball player! He took me inside. They left me alone then. He must have been my angel—smile-to God. They kept on Tony until the security people fought their way to him. Job Corps was nice, but the people were bad. If I'd stayed I could have a nice job instead a scrubbin' these floors. But the education wasn't worth my life.

My older brothers came to pick me up. When they put my suitcase in the trunk I saw they had their shotguns. They had come ta get me—<u>my</u> brothers. I was so happy. They really cared about me. They were so much older than me, but I didn't know they cared until then. They were good men, my brothers. The basketball player was a good man too. I hope he made it onto a team, I do."

Photo #8: the baseball diamond at Riverside Park in South Baltimore. This is the scene of the next account, given at the scene, by an eye-witness, from the vantage he witnessed it; the same vantage from which this photo was taken. As of 2006 the average annual *individual* income in this neighborhood was $101,000. This is not the ghetto, despite the trash strew about the park.

When You're Food

The Substitutes

#30-01-02: day, minutes, eye-witness

"I was playin' basketball with some friends on the court here while the softball league played on the field; a mixed-race regular team against an all black replacement team. It turned out that the replacement team never signed the book and nobody knew who they were! They had brought their lawn-chairs, wives, girlfriends. So you figure, gee whiz, they might be from a bad area, but there ain't gonna be no violence. But after they lost the first game—lost real bad to the regular team—one a the guys on the court said, 'Somethin's gonna break out.'

The replacements was losin' the second game bad too. I was dribblin' the ball, had my back to everybody and everybody started runin' and there was a commotion. I turnt around and the black team was grabbin' their bats and goin' after the mixed-race team. Just about the whole team had their bats and was waylayin' anybody from the other team they could get to—en the women, it was like they was cheer-leadin' them on! They didn't get involved, but they were havin' a good ole time.

The replacements had been fieldin' and all their bats were in bags up against the fence on the first-base side where their women was. The first to grab a bat and attack was the first-baseman; a

gorilla, six-one three-twenty. He didn't need a bat—
just wanted to make sure. He took out after the
first base coach, who was a pretty big guy. The first-
base coach was all alone separated from his team,
and only made it to the pitcher's mound. The gorilla
was swinging down and over—diagonal. The little
catcher was up-swinging like he had a golf club, and
three fielders were kicking and stomping him
where he lay. He was waylaid somethin' terrible.

A tall thin black guy from the mixed-race
team was bein' attacked at home plate, and the rest
of his team was scatterin'—except for this small
guy who ran out to help the first-base coach and got
chased over the third-base fence by the gorilla and
the little golf-swinger. I thought he was a gonner.

I thought golly, 'that guy doesn't have a
chance.' I wanted to help. But what was my little
butt gonna do? I used to watch Planet of the Apes
on TV and that's what it looked like—the gorilla
soldiers with the night sticks! I held onto the fence
and yelled, 'Stop!' and they all stopped, grabbed
their stuff and ran passed me to their cars. They
must have thought I said, 'Cops!' The guys on the
court walked over to the street-side fence and one
of the replacements had a gun and said, 'Back off.'

The umpire called the paramedics on the
first-base coach's cell phone. His wife was there
tendin' to him on the mound. But they didn't come
for half an hour, and had to be re-routed around the
park. The police took forty-five minutes. It was the
most terrible thing I ever saw. The first-base coach

was the only one hurt bad. His leg didn't work right and his one eye was hangin' out to the side."

Yebits
#59-04: night, minutes, first-person defender

"I was twenty-two, five-eleven, a hundred-and-eighty pounds. My name Yebits, is a made up word that means 'The Ugly One' that I had from school. I was working as a mill operator at Grumman Aircraft. I had wrecked my car the night before; broke my nose, and was busted up pretty bad, and had gone out with a friend to kill some pain.

It was after closing and we were crossing North Point toward the K-mart to get breakfast at Denny's. Me and my buddy Donald—a small guy—were standing on the side of the road and this guy in a van yelled, 'Get out of the road.'

I yelled, 'Fuck you! I'll take you all on!'

Didn't think much of it. They were doin' about forty. We were just about in Denny's when Donald said, 'There's a wall of people behind us. We better run.'

I was like, 'Oh man, we'll be alright.'

We were close to the door when I heard, 'Get the big one.'

When I turned around I caught a beer bottle across the nose—knocked the broken nose to the other side of the face—and beer splashed in my eyes. I really couldn't see after that. I swung three times and missed. They could see me comin'. I felt hands on my arms, head, body—bunch of people pushing me to the ground.

Donald had four on him. He got hit in the gonads and ran in increasingly wider circles until he broke away and ran across North Point to find this cop he had seen. There had been seven on me: eleven fucking hicks in that van; a country music concert or some shit had emptied out. Now there was another vehicle-load, a pickup truck. So there's four more. I got eleven people around me kicking; if you can get eleven people around a guy in a fetal position.

I got up and got punched back down. I was covering and screaming out, 'Let me up and I'll take you one at a time!'

I specifically remember this one guy with pointy boots trying to kick me in the face. I was making a muscle to protect my face. He kicked me in the bicep about twenty times and finally got through—broke my jaw. I was getting fuzzy—can't remember much after that.

Donald got to the cop. When she pulled up they were gone. She asked, me if I wanted to press charges. I said, 'Against who lady? Do you see anybody here?'

She was very rude and wasn't even going to give me a ride home—didn't want me bleeding on her car. When I woke up the next morning I had both eyes swollen shut, left ear was cut, nose was pushed over to the right side, bruised from head-to-toe front-and-back, and had a couple of broken ribs on the right side.

I saw Donald the next day. He had a swollen eye. I was a little pissed at him. He said he did all he could to get the cop. I can't blame the guy. I didn't realize that there was so many and that they would do what they did, that they were out for blood. They would have killed me if he hadn't been there. I think they knew the cop was there and knew where he was headed when he broke free."

Group-on-group Postscript [1974]

Since age 11 I have known that weak groups draw strong groups like a magnet draws nails. One late-summer day five of us little guys were engaged in an apple fight with a similar number of pre-teens from a rival neighborhood on the grounds of Babcock Presbyterian Church, in Loch Raven Village, Baltimore County. This was next to the house of a wealthy bachelor, whose college-age sons used the mansion as a frat house. They had an apple tree in their yard which we raided for ammunition to fuel our petty war.

While we were center-field tossing apples at our adversaries, over a dozen long-haired men came out onto the driveway which led to the wooded property around the house they partied at. They directed their fire at our enemies who had their backs to the fence. The apples were thrown with such velocity that they splattered on the fence and actually knocked some kids out. We cheered with glee as our giant allies mowed down the enemy. Then, after the route of our opponents, the men turned their pitching arms on us, which, in retrospect, I must admit were impressive for a bunch of pot-smoking hippies.

Billy went down with bruised ribs, unable to breathe. My brother Tony was hit square between the shoulder blades trying to get to me and was knocked flat on his face, the wind driven from his lungs. Joey was struck on the forehead and knocked out cold, applesauce between his eyes. Somehow I was missed. I managed to drag Joey and Tony back behind the brush-pile, which we used as our fort, while the men thudded the last of the apples into poor Billy, who was still trying to crawl home. Only the minister's son was spared. The rest of us never even hung out together again. It wasn't safe. I spent about six months stalking the smallest of these college hippies and eventually caught him in an alley. But that was the best we could manage, terrorizing their emaciated mascot when he was alone.

Reality Check

Of the dozens of participants above only three were arrested, all of them defenders. Really, what validity can law-enforcement statistics have? Also, who above has been protected by the police?

Chapter 7

Cops & Vigilantes

"You don't know how disappointed I was when I realized you were an employee. When I first spotted you on surveillance I said, 'Man, this dirt-bag looks hungry! I'm beating some ass tonight!'

Then I saw you pushing that U-boat, and I'm like, "Shit, just another degenerate night-crew guy."

-Ed "The Enforcer", career security guard

I did manage some law-enforcement interviews. Law-enforcement situations share some predatory aspects, but generally fall outside of this study. Much of the following material is heavily edited to protect the cops—and well, the author, from the cops. The vigilante action, on the other hand, equals or surpasses the violence of the material in the last chapter. The primary purpose of including this chapter is that police and vigilante actions are socially acceptable—especially the vigilante action. I put it here to serve as a counterbalance to the aloneness and chaos that permeates the rest of this book.

When You're Food

Talking to the Cops

Joe

"Look man, when I talk to you I'm anonymous. I could lose my job for talking to you. Why do people fight the cops? Because a lot of cops need their butts beaten. I see it, the way my fellow officers talk to people like they're trash. A little respect goes a long way. But that's too much to ask of some of these guys. Too many of them want to be Bruce Willis whacking the bad guys.

The bad thing about fighting the cops is that we keep on coming; two at a time, until you lose. Why anyone would fight a cop on a rational basis is beyond me. But if you have an aggressive American—I mean how many people did our ancestors kill to get this place? It's in our blood—drunk, getting hassled by some bully in uniform, I can see the basis for some violence. I'll get you after you commit a crime, not because you look like the guy that's dating the girl that dumped me.

As a cop the encounter is stacked in my favor. My backup outnumbers yours. I've got the toys: cruiser, vest, gun, stick, mace—radio! My partner never got in a fight his whole life until he became a city cop. Now he fights all the time and loves it. To me though, if I take the proper precautions, I'm not fighting so much as I'm managing violence. A win for me is no casualties on either side. Now, if you really want to talk violence you need to interview some corrections officers. Those guys have to deal with everything we bring them. We bring them trouble one at a time. They're with all the trouble at the same time. I wouldn't want that job."

Jerald

"The juveniles are the worst. I saw one knock out an adult inmate at The Facility (Baltimore City Central Booking). We get it all. One of 'em fought three of us over his phone privileges. He picked up a three-hundred-pound officer! Weren't more than one-sixty hisself. He almost hit my partner with a milk crate. We beat 'im down with the radios. We're not permitted to carry weapons on The Inside so we use the radio.

Once three of us were escorting this juvenile and he punches my partner. The nose explodes. He's down. I'm on the floor holding his legs and the other officer is working 'im with the radio until two more officers come. There was eventually thirteen of us. We beat 'im and stomped 'im three at a time—it was tiring. When we finished his head looked like this (points to knuckles of right fist).

Infirmary shit! He hurt a guard en put hisself there to begin with. Three-thousand of them and five-hundred of us. We all black. Brutha this, brutha that. Fuck 'em! They don't fuck with the guards at Hagerstown (State Facility in Rural Western Maryland): all yessir, nosir up there. They know not ta fuck with those white-boys; know what they'll get! Why should it be any different down here?"

When You're Food

Mac

"The worst beating I ever took was from a black girl, back when I was still in uniform. I was reeling out of there, blood running off me, radio dangling. It was unreal...

On the East Side last night there was a stabbing. I work undercover in Narcotics on the West Side, and I'm thinking, they're still stabbing people over there? Who is still doing that? Two Mexican guys, that's who. Once my training officer and I got a call to a bar fight on the East Side. We walk in and this Lumbee is working this folding dirk knife—double-edged, prohibited by the Annotated Code of Maryland, only good for one thing—really working it. We thought we weren't going to make it out of there. He got his—a night stick in the face knocked half his teeth out.

I grew up in D.C. All you heard about down there was police brutality. I had just graduated from the university, and had interviewed with the FBI, and I'm thinking to myself, 'What am I doing getting involved with a city police department; getting caught up in all the brutality and corruption?'

By-and-large I have to say that I've been pleased with the (police) behavior. People call it brutality. But with violent people there are certain levels of force that are part of the job. There are some officers who go over the edge. There is brutality and I've seen it. I've taken down cops in my work with Narcotics. I've been involved in police kidnappings, where the guy is taken to a park and stripped down. But there is not a lot of police brutality in Baltimore.

Never forget the element you are dealing with, the dummies out there buying this stuff. Most do become statistics. I've been on a thousand raids. We hit the door ourselves. In seven out of ten there is someone in there who doesn't want you there— there grabbing for a gun or a knife, or fighting you. People on the outside don't realize what it's like in West Baltimore, what a war-zone it is. I have whole file boxes of gang members by their street names— the names are just too much. You don't have to go looking for these people. Just stand out on North Avenue and they will find you."

Miles

"This guy was trouble—and wasn't too smart. He called my supervisor, after I whacked him in the leg with the ASP trying to arrest him, claiming he was his brother and that I had broke his brother's leg. We could tell it was him. He was a real low-life: child-support; armed robbery; burglary; auto-theft. He got taken down by ten city cops. He fought them and they beat the shit out of him. How do you reason with somebody like that? What an idiot! You really think you're going to beat ten cops? Really?

A lot of guys that fight cops are really just pussies. They know that the cops will hold back— it's not like we're out there trying to kill you."

Fighting the Cops!

Ricky

"I got in a fight with a cop on the corner over there. I was drunk. He was doing his job. I beat him fair and square. When we went to court he even said a good word for me to the judge. I liked him after that.

I was young...seventeen. On PCP. Me and some friends wanted a drink so we broke into this bar after hours. They left. But I sat up on the bar and drank until the cops tried to arrest me. It took four of 'em. I wrestled in school and boxed. I loved to fight—still do, just hurts more now. They worked me with blackjacks. That's how they did you. They eventually cuffed me.

When I was an adult, two of 'em tried to arrest me in that alley over there. They couldn't do it, even with the blackjacks—PCP. Two more came, couldn't do it. After a while there was six. They finally beat me down and made the arrest. My brother saw them working over a friend one time and he tried to help. They—four of them—beat him. They killed him."

Puppet

"It was a drug bust. We were all sittin' at the Geno's. A friend of ours had sold to a Narc. They had been watching the place. When Danny left ten or eleven cars pulled in, and all these Narcs got out and chased him—took him down.

When You're Food

They were plain clothes and showed no badges. My brother was getting beat up. They had brought the dogs out and were getting ready to let them loose on him because he wouldn't stop fightin'. That's when I went out.

I jumped on top of this cop, wrapped my legs around his waist, grabbed his hair in both hands, and started shaking his head—trying to tear it off! He really couldn't do anything because I was on his back. I had a ball! It was a lot of fun; me beatin' up a guy instead of getting' beat up by a guy. I was yelling, 'You fucking pig. Get off my brother!'

He was yelling, 'Get this bitch off me!'

The other cops told me that if I didn't let go they were going to let the dogs loose. They got me down and cuffed me. They put me in a separate car from the guys and cuffed me to a chair at the station. The lady cop that searched my purse found my pot, and put it back in and didn't say anything. In court the cop said that I gave him the worst headache of his life and that I was a wild woman. I was sixteen. They all got probation. I got off."

Justice

Monando Cay

"I fly in (to Caracas Venezuela) from da big island (Jamaica) to pick up sometin'. It was a rainy day (smacks lips in disgust) mud, cold. The car not so good. I stop for directions at dis small place; a

138

few buildings here and there, where two roads cross. Many evil Spanish men standing about wearing hats. I rise from dis little (smacks lips in disgust) car en dis boy—thirteen perhaps—come running out from dis market with a can of corn. Da owner follow, waiving a towel, yelling.

Every mon on dat street draw gun—all of dem! Little gun, big gun, long gun—two gun! Many, many gun. Such gun! Dey shoot dat boy down in street—in mud, for <u>one</u> can corn. I turn around, do not stop until airport."

Vernon

"I was baggin' groceries at the market... A commotion outside... I go out en there is two big young dudes holding this bum and punchin' 'im. I go to break it up en dis dude grabs me, 'No, don't, he stole their mamma's money', and point across the street ta Miss Bess standin' on 'er porch, leanin' on the railin' shakin' 'er fist in da air. So I'm like yeah, 'Kick his ass!!!!'

His face swelled some en they tossed 'im. Them boys kicked that dude all the way down to the street en toe-kicked 'is face in the gutter until he was just a limp bag a meat. The dudes lifted their mamma's money off the body en went back across the street. It was alright man. While they walked her back over to the market so she could buy her groceries there was cheerin', back-slappin', hugs, hand-shakes.

I think the cops eventually scraped up the bum. We had forgot about him."

When You're Food

Baby Girl

"This was up on Baltimore Street, summer, Saturday Night. I'm at the bus stop and this pretty light-skinned girl—who is pregnant, starting to show—is coming out of the club with her friends. These three weed-heads—one being the baby's fatha—pull up in a Land Cruiser and begin yelling at her for clubin' while she pregnant. Her friends tried to shield her but the baby's fatha grabbed her by her tracks (hair extensions) and began bangin' her in her face and screaming that she should be home. When she said something back he hit her again, and his friends said, 'You didn't have to do that.'

The girl walk off, and the weed-heads park and sat up on a parking lot wall, whistlin' at girls, braggin' 'bout they bad selves, like they was somethin'.

Fifteen minutes later, my ass is still waitin' on the damn One en these three weed-heads are still camped out there, getting high and callin' at girls, acting like they own the street. Then two vehicles pull up in front: a black BMW and a beater, and this really tall dude with dreads and a trench-coat pulls up on a mo-ped behind the weed-heads in the parking lot.

Four dudes got out of the BMW : a big thick dude in fine threads; a tall buff dude in fine threads; a small mean dude wearing a jacket; and another little dude. Out of the beater stepped this oh-my-

God-sexy dude. He pulled the light-skinned girl
from the car and said, 'Where the niggas at?'

She pointed at the stupid weed-heads sitting
on that parking lot wall with their feet dangling off
the ground.

The gorgeous dude—he was very finely
dressed and I think was her brother—snapped his
fingers and the buff dude and thick dude walked up
on either side, while he grabs the guy and says, 'Is
this the one? Is this the nigga?!'

She just jumped back in the car—no answer.
He grabs the the nigga off the wall with both hands,
spits in his face, and says, 'You ain't shit, beatin' on
a girl who is pregnant. We'll show you how we treat
bitchez!'

His friends just sat there in shock while he
threw him down. Then the buff dude and the thick
dude kicked and stomped his ass for maybe five
minutes, while the mean little guy in the jacket beat
him in his head with one of those souvenir baseball
bats. He was just cryin' and coverin'. After a while
the sexy dude signals them to stop, and somebody
says, 'Yo, are we gonna take him to da lake?'

The sexy dude said, 'Let's roll', and they all
rolled off.

Everybody that was watching was laughin' so
hard they was cryin'. And then the two stupid
friends, standin' over the body, start talkin' tough
like they was about ready to step in. All the girls
started yelling insults, and one girl walks up and
says, 'Ya all best take this nigga to the hospital
'cause I know his head is fucked up!'

When You're Food

They lay him in the back of the Land Cruiser and drov

Chapter 8

Convergence Predation

"No arts; no letters, no society; and which is
worst of all, continual fear and danger of violent
death; and the life of man, solitary, poor, nasty,
brutish and short.'
-Thomas Hobbes

Mister Hobbes nailed early Twenty-first
Century Baltimore. Black men born in Baltimore
City only have a 48-year life expectancy. That is
medieval. Just as herbivores on the African
savannah are in most peril when they go to the
watering-hole, modern Americans are most in
jeopardy when they go shopping, or frequent any
other location where the hunters of humans
converge to satiate their hunger.

As a supermarket manager, and as a security
manager for card tournaments, I have much
experience playing sheep-dog verses the wolves
that prey on my customers as if they are the sheep
in a brutal fairy tale. In this role I have had good
experiences with the police. Police forces, as
organized, are no good at protecting individuals.
They are however, highly useful for the protection
of businesses, and hence the businesses' clientele. If

thugs are trying to crash into your house, the cops are a half-hour away. If these same thugs harass your customers, the cops show in ten minutes, and they back you up!

There are three types of convergence predation: byway, event, and facility.

Byway Predation

From 10:45 a.m. to 12:45 p.m., of Friday, December 31st, 1999 I was stalked by a uniformed police officer. He followed me, waited for me, harassed me, accused me, questioned me, threatened me, and continued to follow me after I finally told him I had just come back into town for my paycheck. It then occurred to me that he might rob me. I worked with some Mexican guys who routinely got robbed by cops. I saw him take up a blocking position on Fort Avenue and knew I had to find an alternative way out of there. I lucked out. Three women that I worked with were getting off work and invited me out for a drink. I'm not a drinker. But, I reasoned, 'Better to be drunk under the table by these savage little beasts and have them roll me out of their car in front of my wife four hours from now, than to serve as the bad guy in Officer RayBob's autobiography'. Officer RayBob had his brand-new night-stick leaning against the backrest in his passenger seat as if it were a much-loved pet!

Most of the advice on avoidance and evasion that I have dispensed over the course of this series of books has been based on my extensive experience as the target of byway predation. I see no sense in beating it to death here. The following incidents I collected recently from friends.

Tim

"You know, I'm old now, didn't figure on having to fight for my money anymore. I was transferring from the One to the Fifteen uptown and these three white dudes—early thirties—kept asking me for money. I said, 'Brother, I don't have any money.' Then the punches came. I gave back, hit one a couple, and managed to back down Saratoga. They did not pursue. Guess I can still crack a little. Guess I was lucky. But I was banged–up too. The wife wouldn't let me head out to the day job anymore after that. Hopefully when I beat this pneumonia I'll find a second job closer to home."

JimBob

"This was in August of O-seven. Walkin' home after a pit-stop at the bar for beer and reefer, heading up the right side of White at Bella Vista, where that [grassy] lot is. Six or seven section-eight teenagers are running across the field yelling, 'What you got in your wallet yo?'

I didn't even know if they were talking to me. Then I'm smacked in the back of the head. I'm yelling at the top of my lungs. There was significant traffic. No one stopped to drive me out or even call the cops. They kept circling, trying to knock me down with punches—only punching from behind. This continued for at least five minutes, maybe ten.

These are fourteen to fifteen year-old kids. I'm yelling the entire time, and no one even looks out of a window. Of course, they all came out to walk their dogs as soon as it was over.

A seventh shows up, a little older, eighteen or nineteen. About twenty feet away he holds up a gun [over his shoulder] and yells, 'Enough of this shit!'

I think he was ready to shoot them if it continued.

I get plucked in the head from behind and I cuss the kid, and the gunman says, 'Chill out. What else you got in your pocket?'

He's got the gun down by his hip now. I said, 'Keys, wallet, reefer.'

He said, 'Give it up.'

They got the whole wallet—I'D' and all—fifteen dollars in cash, and forty in reefer. I handed it off to one of the younger kids and they walked off. Now I'm walking up the street in a rage yelling, 'Welcome to the fuckin' hood. You wanted section-eight housing. You got it you liberal motherfuckers!'

This young guy poked his head out the window up the street and asked me what was the matter. He brought me a beer—the best tasting honey wheat I ever had—and let me use his phone to call the police. When I was a kid we used to go after other kids, but never families or adults. That has changed."

Event Predation

My experience with this comes via the bizarre world of collectable trading card tournaments. All I know about the actual game is that it is a racket. The player buys his own deck card-by-card, of which there are thousands, not just 52. The company produces rare cards with special properties which can be valued as high as $2,000 each. What you end up with is 300 geeks with backpacks, containing entire collections, often valued over $5,000, milling around an auditorium for 12 hours. All of this soft high-profit prey attracts its own specific kind of predator. Here is the breakdown.

On the inside is a mixed-race group of 300 potential robbery victims. Out of these 300 2 will have their bags snatched while they are looking the other way, and one will be pack-attacked by a group of large, young black men while the event clears. As security, the primary challenge is cracking the predator's intelligence network. These criminals all play the game. They are smart guys. As robbers go they are not so brutal. They want soft targets that are confirmed to be high-value. Towards this end they plant scouts among the players, and send in scouts to pose as spectators.

Your secondary challenge is crowd control, because the packs emerge out of the crowd, and are actually players. The most important aspect of crowd control is team work. You cannot do this effectively alone. The second most important aspect is identification: you have to wrist-band these people. On this one occasion I was alone and had to begin clearing the room. I started at the back, with a table of loud, large black men—actual ghetto guys—who averaged twice my size and half my age. The leader weighed 570 pounds and required two chairs. These players are so big that tournament organizers have had to face the logistical dilemma known as "chair-melting" as folding metal chairs fail by the dozen beneath these enormous posteriors. What follows is the dialog from my eviction of these over-fed card-sharks:

"Hey guys, time to go—clearing the room, starting at the back, which means starting with you; unless any of you made it to the championship round."

"Yo, I think this is some racist shit! What about all them?"

"They go next, unless they play in the last round—excuse me. I'll be right back..."

Time elapsed: 5 minutes.

"...Okay guys, I've got some good news and some bad news. The good news is I just tossed out four white-boys, a gay dude, a Hispanic dude, some kind of Middle-Eastern dude, and a chick who was not actually ugly. The bad news is I can't find a single Asian kid who isn't playing in the final round. What's up with that?"

"Ah man, why jou have ta go there? That shit's jus' wrong yo. Sides iz cold ouside."

"Well, I understand you refined gentlemen not wanting to wait outside for your little Asian friends to finish winning this thing. However, you all appear to be adequately insulated against the cold; and, I will make you this personal guarantee: if any of these ninety-pound Asian kids attack you and try to take your possessions, I shall protect you. How 'bout that?"

"Ah mannn, you a wrong somebody. We're goin'. But this shit be wrong."

"Thank you gentlemen. Your cooperation is very much appreciated. Excuse me, but I' m going to go and see if I can find an Eskimo—never tossed one of those out before."

"That man is a dick! Yo, lez jus' step from dis joint..."

There you go. Just sit a bouncer at the door and be a dick for 12 hours. That pretty much gets it done.

Facility Predation

This fits the water-hole model perfectly. Your customers are the herbivores. The bums, shop-lifters, panhandlers, purse-snatchers, muggers, and armed robbers are the vultures, jackals, hyenas, cheetahs, leopards and lions. My experience in this area involves supermarkets. Supermarkets are complex facilities that serve a high volume of customers. As a store manager I personally took care of the following assortment of issues, taken from my security log for the weekend of 5/27/10 thru 5/31/10:

5/27: A man was speaking to a cashier using foul sexually-explicit language. I approached him, put a hand on his shoulder, and said, "Shut up.

Apologize. Shut up again. Pay. Do not come back."
On the way out he asked me if he could come back,
and I said, "Yes."

5/27: An elderly man was screaming
obscenities at my courtesy clerk. I took his walker
away, made him lean on his cart, chewed him out,
and got his butter pecan ice cream for him. He
apologized, thanked me, asked me for some
mayonnaise, and checked out peacefully. I gave his
walker back.

5/28: I chased a violent panhandler across
the front parking lot.

5/29: I talked a low-pressure panhandler
away from the storefront.

5/29: I attempted to talk an aggressive
panhandler away from the store front. When he
threatened me I dialed 911 on the cell and he
evaporated.

5/30: I walked an aggressive panhandler
away from the store front.

5/30: I chased a violent panhandler away
from the storefront.

5/30: I chased a bicycle-mounted drug-
dealer off the side parking lot.

5/30: I moved a mo-ped from the
handicapped ramp after the owner refused to move
it.

5/30: I informed an illegal cab-driver
("hacker") that he could not loiter on the side-walk.

5/30: I barred John the Bum from the
property, again.

When You're Food

5/31: At 7:10 p.m., 10 minutes after closing, a drunk tried to force and threaten his way into the store to buy some onions. I called the police when the man would not leave the exiting customers alone. (I had to stay at the door to let people out.) The police officer came at 8:18 p.m., and said, "Next time call it in as an assault. I'll get here quicker."

Most people don't even consider this security work, because I wasn't packing a gun and beating people up. The important thing to remember is that real security work does not consist of kicking ass. Real security work consists of incrementally imposing your will on The Scum of the Earth. Because, if you do not impose your will upon them, they will impose their will upon your customers, and those good people will go shop elsewhere. Remember that the panhandler will morph into a mugger. If he's begging you he's robbing grandma.

Security for a retail facility is also a two-man job. With event security you want a rover and a doorman. At a retail facility you need a detective and manager at minimum. In a bad location you may also need a uniformed guard and an armed police officer. If you find yourself arranging for security for a retail food outlet, here is your checklist of concerns, which amounts to a cascade of liability:

1. You must protect your customers and employees on the storefront and parking lot.
2. You must protect your customers and employees in the store.

3. You must protect your product from opportunistic and professional shoplifters.
4. You must protect your product from thieving employees.
5. You must prevent your employees from conducting illegal operations, such as drug deals, loan sharking, acts of prostitution, and passing counterfeit bills on the property.
6. You must protect your cash from everybody.
7. You must protect your under-aged female customers from the sexual advances of your store detective.
8. You must protect your female employees from the sexual advances of your security staff, janitors and assistant managers; mostly the security staff.
9. You must protect the company from slip-and-falls. Almost every customer fantasizes about slipping on a banana peel and suing you for a million bucks. So picking up that trash that your janitor and store-detective missed while they were feeling up the office girl is probably your most important task.

When you are lucky enough to get a good security man at your retail facility, you want to keep him, and interview him of course...

Kenneth
#57-24: night, seconds, first-person aggressor
"Was headed up front the store en there two of 'em; tall, thin, young hoppers, behine the register

with the cashier—en she scared. I tell Allan ta call Baltimore County en I on the case sure enough. I walk up and say, 'Security.'

The sidekick say, 'Security ain't shit!'

The otha boy got 'is right 'and in 'is pocket like he got somethin', and put 'is otha hand on the back a the cashier's neck, like to push her to the register. That when he fuck up!

The produce man come up front with the mop-handle ready ta go. I take off my security hat—ain't the man no more—en say, 'This ain't about The Company nigga. You put a hand on my woman! It personal now!'

I en the produce man there ready ta rumble and the nigga makin' like he got somethin' in 'is pants. But he don't pull it.

'Well nigga, if you got it, pull it! I one a those hard-headed niggas. I gots ta see it! I don't see no gun nigga, then we gonna roll!'

They not wanna roll with us. So they run off to a getaway car drove by a woman."

#58-19 to 22: minutes, aggressor/defender/eye-witness

"It was July in Edmondson Village—in the hood, about Eight-thirty at night. I spotted this one young hopper—twenty-six, twenty-seven—fillin' 'is backpack with bottles of lotion. He run en I grab 'is bag—en it on! I was beatin' 'is ass—goin' ta work—when I felt someone jump on top of me from behine en hit me in the back of the head. I was a sandwich on the floor. But I was battlin', keepin' a hold a that bag—a hundred-en-twenty dollars worth a merchandise in that bag.

I had ta regroup—yelled for the girls to call nine-one-one. You could hear them hollerin', 'Mister Kenny fightin'!' I was fightin' two guys en they was tearin' my ass up! I told 'em, 'You might win the fight, but you gonna lose the battle. Ya'll bes' give it up, 'cause when the cavalry get here it ass whoopin' time—not throw-yo-ass-up-against-the-wall time, but <u>ass whoopin'</u> time!'

Yesssir, put you hands on a guard and you askin' for the baton. I don't fear the enemy, en I don't surrender, 'cause the police be ma posse, en they be a comin'.

The guy on the bottom says, 'Let's kill this muthafuca!'

That's when I started losin' track a time. It must a been minutes. Three cashiers jump on top a the guy that on top a me. So I got four people on my back—getting' too old for this. They was young teen girls. Did pretty good for bein' girls—broke them store-bought nails they had.

When the first guy got off me I knew they had come. Police hit him with his stick and knocked him off my back. Then I jumped off the guy I was on—let the police handle them. There was four cops; three guys en a girl. We took them in the back and they whoopin' the dog-shit out'a them. Then they called the ambulance, and by that time they needed it.

When the ambulance got there they let them lay and looked after me. The only thing I los' was a tooth en a little bit a pride. But I got my pride back when they took 'em out on the stretchers."

#54-09 to 14: night, minutes, defender, witness

"It was Eight-o-Five, Thursday night, Edmondson Village. These two young drug-addicted hoppers in there with a bag actin' like they come to buy somethin'. I made them leave. They come back, fill the bag up with bodywash, en try ta run. I grab one en he hit me right in the mouth—it on!

I go to pull ma mace en the otha hopper come up from behine en grab it. I go for the stick en the hopper in front knock it out a ma hand. I was battlin' fo ma life—fightin' two niggers at one time. We was battlin' on the floor. I was getting' whooped, but given too; use the handcuffs as brass knuckles.

Somebody said, 'Mister Kenny fightin'. Call nine-one-one.'

This fool girl call the police, en then call ma daughter, who call ma sons, who call their friends from the hood. Meanwhile I got help: a lady customer and four register girls on these hoppers, tryin' ta dig me out, en battlin' 'till the cavalry come. I was bareback when the whole mess of us crash through the glass at the front of the store, en we battlin' on the lot, blood everywhere and one a these hoppers bitin' me.

The cops roll up, en they lend a hand. A police knock this one hopper off me with a two-handed stick stroke under the chin, which take him off his feet. Two more cops roll up en we out of it. The police workin' the dog-shit out'a them; kickin', stompin', bustin' knees. Eventually they get them in the van. Then ma boys show up. I said, 'Oh Lord, why'd you have ta call them girl. Never call my boys when I battlin', can be unreasonable.'

Cars roar up, en ten of 'em get out. I weren't hurt bad but I looked a mess. Ma oldest boy walk to the cops en say, 'Where the nigga that put a hand on my daddy?'

The cop said, 'We can't let you have 'im.'

That when the guns come out. Four cops en ten niggas with guns! The cops callin' for backup, en the head cop turn to me, en say, 'I don't get paid enough for this shit!'

The boys are rockin' the paddy wagon, tryin' to break in, while their hoodlum friends en the cops are in a standoff. Backup started rollin' in quick: Metro Police; Housing Police; more City cops, en a tactical squad.

The boys friends with the guns roll out. But ma boys were still tryin' to break into the van, en had to be dispersed with tear gas. One officer said, 'Sorry we had o hit one sir.'

The paramedics took care a me, and the hoppers were charged with theft, felony assault and trespassing. I got time off with pay, and the boss come to my house. But I gettin' too old."

Chapter 9

Goodnight Harm City

"Welcome to Harm City."
-Grafitti by Kaos Krew artist on #15 Bus,
Baltimore, MD, 2000

This chapter is nothing more than my goodbye to Baltimore. It was originally written in four segments in early 2000, as I was also saying goodbye to the violence study I had been pursuing since 1996, in favor of a subject that could be researched in the quiet confines of a library. I have added the fifth segment as a postscript.

Photo #9: The business card the author gave to those he interviewed, and on at least one occasion, to an armed robber, who decided he needed a biographer more than he needed $18 in cash.

ACTION BIOGRAPHY
by
JAMES LaFOND, "The Violence Guy"
True Tales Of:
Survivors • Fighters
Veterans • Adventurers
& Security Professionals

- Paladin Press -
P.O. Box 1307, Boulder, CO 80306

The Interview
Monday, January 17, 2000, 9:00 p.m., Harford & Southern, #19 Bus Stop, Northeast Baltimore

The wind-chill is well below zero, and I had misread the bus schedule for the Martin Luther King holiday. My reverie on civic transportation—not to mention my foul mood—is interrupted by a 15-year-old boy walking up to me, his hands in the front pockets of his hoody. The metal streetlight pole is behind me. The curb is one foot to my right.

He is just to my left. I'm sick of being hunted and harassed by packs of these little monsters. I immediately become overwhelmed with the urge to kill him. Images of cutting off his little head and bowling over the malt liquor bottles in the gutter with it flash across my darkening mind's eye...

"Yo, you got fifty cents?"

"*Yes!*"

My enemy hesitates, gathers his courage, and moderates his approach, "Can I have it?"

"*Nooo!*"

We make hard eye-contact as he fades back to his right off behind my left shoulder and clutches more fiercely at whatever is in his pocket. He is getting angry, "You didn't have to say it like that!"

"No, I didn't have to say it *like that!*"

I begin turning towards him and take a step forward to keep the distance close so I can stab him. He reads this and backs up quickly down Southern, keeping the pole between us. He reaches under his hoody and starts digging for something in the waistband of his sweat pants, as he continues to break away and I stand my ground, "Yo mothafuca, come 'ere. I got somethin' fo ya. I'll bus' a cap in yo ass!"

He continues to back away up Southern and is soon lost out of sight behind a building. As his voice fades, and I am the only thing left on the street I hear something. It's me. I'm snarling like an animal. A half-hour later I am on a deserted bus rumbling downtown, wondering if my research— my constant consideration of violence, and hours of daily interviews with violent criminals and their victims—is beginning to warp my mind.

The Pack

An hour after failing the robbery interview, I am on the corner of Light and Pratt at the Inner Harbor waiting on the #1 Bus, across from Jos. A. Banks Clothiers, where the smoking-hot rich chick for whom I serve alternately as escort and houseboy, purchases the outfits that she dresses my up in. My reflections on my secret life as a man-whore are interrupted by a serenely normal scene; two young couples window shopping in front of the closed upscale urban outfitter. These are two really pretty young white women escorted by two tall handsome young men, one white, one mixed.

Samson, a cripple veteran, who is panhandling in his wheel chair, flips over in a pothole in the bus lane. I manage to get him back in his seat and up on the walk. As I'm returning his sock full of change to him he nods across the street and say, "Look at this shit."

I turn to see a pack of three young black men swooping down on the two couples, executing a running attack in echelon (one flank refused). The girls are the target. When the fast little twerps dart past their men and punch them on the run, they go down in weeping shrieking heaps behind the men.

A second wave of three homeboys throw their running punches at the men who are backing up with balled-up women under their feet, and go down on top of the women as they are struck.

When You're Food

Now a third wave of four attackers comes running in and stays on station for about ten seconds, punching the four well-dressed young people. The big studly guys, who each appeared to be a match for any three of these little barbarians, are completely overwhelmed.

Now a fourth wave, of only two young men, swoops in and punches the pile of men and women, dancing around like fiends, and then run off.

Samson and a nurse get on the #64 Bus headed to Harbor Hospital. Across Light Street victims are crying to and consoling one another. A minute later I roll out to Locust Point on the #1 Bus. I'm now questioning my ability to protect my 10-year-old son, who can only leave the house with me as an escort. His mother has been locked in doors for six-months in our Northeast Baltimore row home, afraid to leave the house after being beaten up on the #19 Bus by two black women, and then followed home by two black men, who I chased off with a tomahawk.

I say to myself, "LaFond, you're taking her out to dinner, and you will kill anyone who threatens her."

I am going over the edge. I no longer think in terms of defense or avoidance or protection. I only think about killing the ubiquitous enemy. Somewhere within, the tiny vestigial civilized person I used to be is mourning his transmogrification into what he has become; a combative creep who takes his every waking step on the dark streets of Baltimore in anticipation of a fight to the death with someone's teenage sons. I am now completely prepared, indeed planning, to kill one or some of these little barbarians. I do not, though, wish to go to prison.

So I decided to stop carrying knives, on that fateful night. At break time I began practicing on the cardboard bails in the stockroom with various ink pens. I found that the Bic penetrated up to three inches but shattered on hard surfaces. The Papermate only got an inch of penetration and bent rather than shattered. To this day I arm myself with 1 to 3 pens anytime I go outside. I like the Bic as a primary, with two Papermates, in various draw positions, for backup. If I am headed to work I will also permit myself a box-cutter as a backup weapon for clinches and floor fights.

A Smoke
Friday, February 4, 2000, 8:45 p.m., Southern Avenue, Northeast Baltimore
My wife and I are walking home from the last remaining sit-down restaurant in this part of town (It closed a year later.) We are a quarter-mile from home. I have been up for forty hours and am not as alert as usual. (At this point in my life I usually slept 45-minutes every day, and eight hours on my day off.) It is a dark misty night. The sidewalks are covered with four feet of week-old ploughed snow turned to dirty ice. We are walking up the right side of the street in the icy tire rut, headed past Simms and Schley, to Luerssen, our destination.

When You're Food

At Simms we spot two homeboys walking down the left hand side of the street toward us at about Luerssen. She puts out her cigarette and puts on her gloves, expecting a fight. I put my left hand on her shoulder but neglect to get her to my right, a major lapse in judgment.

At the mouth of Schley they both put their hands into the pockets of their starter jackets and say something to one another. They are about to pass on our left. There is a thin guy on the inside, and a muscular guy on the outside. He is the hitter. He says, "Yo' y'all have a cigarette?"

I said nothing and glared at him, establishing hard eye-contact. So long as this eye-contact is not broken he will not escalate. I know this from dozens of these encounters. I have a handle on this. I feel my wife tense up. She panics, and picks up her pace—breaking my eye-contact as she passes between me and the hitter. To make matters worse, she belatedly answers, "No."

The hitter says, "You lie bitch!"

Whoever initiates hard eye-contact has the initiative. I have lost the initiative and must regain it. They are rubbernecking on their toes. She is a big tall girl and I'm having trouble shoving her out of my way on the uneven ice. This is interfering in my closing the distance so I can stab the hitter in the neck. It is also interfering with his view of my hands. I'm not strong enough to push her out of my way with one hand and she is panicking, trying to stay next to me, which is keeping her in danger. I feel like one of the studs on Light and Pratt.

When You're Food

Just as I get my hand into the pocket of my duster and palm the Bic I reestablish eye-contact with the hitter as I push around her, back toward his position. He wolfs, "Yo muthafuca, give me a smoke."

I'm shoving her along in front of me now with the left, looking into his wide eyes over my left shoulder, my hand still in the pocket. His sidekick swallows hard.

The hitter yells, "Yo muthafuca come 'ere."

I stop pushing and turn, take my hand out of the pocket and drop it behind my hip.

His sidekick whispers, "He got a gun yo!"

She is hurrying on now, so I begin to close the distance.

The hitter barks, "Yo muthafuca, come'on. I got a twenny-two fo yo punk-ass!"

As he begins to pull his hands out of his pockets and I flex my legs to run in, his friend grabs his wrists and prevents him from drawing, obviously afraid of being caught in a cross-fire, "No yo, lez roll, he got some shit yo!"

I began backing up the street after my wife as the sidekick push-drags the hitter back into Schley as the hitter continues to wolf, "I gotchyou yo. I got sometin' fo yo punk-ass."

Five-minutes later we are safely inside of our row-home and my wife say, "I don't care what you have to do, but get us out of this fucking city. I'm never leaving this house again until we move."

The Redneck Riviera

For the four years that we lived in Dundalk, before my wife finally fired me, we had fewer and less serious problems. My eleven-year old was once robbed by two 15-year-olds. My wife was mugged by a lone Hispanic guy on the local supermarket parking lot. But she did beat the shit out of him, even stomped him. We were similarly panhandled by a little white twerp with a knife, who I threatened, chased, and cornered in a wooded lot on the riverbank next to a bridge. He looked behind him into the woods and I said, "You can die back in there, with that knife in your hand. Or you can drop that knife and I'll let you cross the bridge."

That knife made it into my youngest son's collection of souvenir knives that his crazy father has taken from people. Aside from fat rednecks in pickup trucks constantly entertaining me by threatening to beat me up, our exodus to that white-trash enclave in Southeastern Baltimore County was a success. My wife and son still live there ten years later while I slum-it in the city.

Silk Man-panties and All
A Tuesday, February, 2001, Light & Pratt, #10
Bus Stop, the Inner Harbor

I am walking uptown, relieved, but kind of hostile. I had just been fired by the smoking-hot rich chick. Well, not exactly fired, I was-laid off. She was moving out of town. She had asked me to keep the thousands of dollars worth of clothes she had purchased for me to wear. When she was going to fly into town for a visit she would call ahead, and let me know what to wear. I promised not to heave them into a dumpster, although I desperately wanted to. I could not though. I was, after all, a man-whore of honor.

I am in a bind, one of pride. I had promised not to throw away the clothes. But, if I go home with these clothes, than my wife will know that I have been dumped by the girlfriend. That is an hour of belly-laughing, finger-pointing, and jokes about man-panties that I am not willing to endure. I am too proud to grant the old lady her moment of laughter at my expense.

As I stalk irritably around the bus shelter I notice this fifty-year-old black dude; a small guy, slightly smaller than I. He is "dressed up": a pink dress shirt with frayed sleeves; a thread-bare plaid bow-tie; gray dress slacks from the 1970's; and those hard leather dress shoes that Mom used to make my brother and I wear every Easter Sunday. The right shoe had a hole, exposing the man's big toe and holey sock.

I'm stepping closer to him, checking him out—even smelling him to make sure he's not homeless. He is getting nervous. He turns, swallows hard, and stammers, "Look man, I ain't got nothin' but this bus ticket. Please don't take that from me. I got a job interview. I can't be late. This might be ma last shot."

"I ain't gonna rob ya man. I was jus' checkin' out yer size, wonderin' if you needed some clothes."

When You're Food

He looks nervously at the large woman's beach bag that I am carrying, looks at my tattered black duster and hair that hasn't been trimmed in twelve years, and protests, "But I ain't got no money man. I'm clean broke. Can' afford no clothes."

"Look man, my girl jus' dumped me. I promised 'er I wouldn't throw this stuff out. But if I show up at ma wife's place with this bag she's gonna laugh in ma face. You can have it. You can have it all: silk shirts; leather shoes I can't pronounce; leopard-skin tank top; silk dress shirts; velvet smokin' jacket; socks with colored spots ta show where yer heel en toe goes; en silk man-panties too. How 'bout it. Jus' take this stuff off ma hands en save me some humiliation?"

"Sure, sure thing mister. Thanks. I got but one set a good clothes and I'm wearin' 'em."

"Yer a pimp now bro."

"Thanks man!"

I have never felt so good. I walk all 14 miles home out into the county, over asphalt humps that used to be rolling hills, just so I can enjoy the feeling of freedom: from the rich chick; my subhuman coworkers; my illiterate boss; my homeboy enemies; and the oppressive trash-heap I've called home for most of my life, and that some idiot politician dubbed "Charm City": Baltimore.

When You're Food

Afterword to the Advance Edition

I employ a number of pre-editorial readers to review my work before I foist it on a publisher. Of course these are folks who have purchased my books and liked them enough to contact me and tell me so. So, it is not exactly like I'm risking massive rejection when I send out my work for review. Largely, I want to make sure I stay in touch with the reading public—or at least my miniscule slice of it—through these people.

Typically I get compliments, questions, ideas and some complaints about not going deep enough here or there. When I sent out *When You're Food* I received an immediate response from all three of those readers indicating that this was far and away the best thing I have written.

My dear mother, having gotten wind of this news, and the fact that a used edition of *The Logic of Steel* has been listed for sale on Amazon at $999.00, has asked to read the manuscript. I responded, "Mom, you have to promise before you read it, that I will not be invited to a family meeting attended by two burly men in white uniforms."

She laughed, made the promise, and then asked, "What is your opinion about that wonderful citizen over in Owings Mills who just got convicted for throwing his little dog off of his third story balcony?"

"Really Mom, he should have thrown his wife off the balcony instead. He wouldn't have gotten in so much trouble."

She then laughed that uncomfortable laugh only ventured by women at once entertained by and worried about their offspring's chances for social acceptance.

So, I am feeling marginally successful, what with copies of my last published book actually selling on line for up to $249.00 and the fact that a senior member of the gentile Scrabble-playing family I was born into is actually willing to subject themselves to my barbarous commentary.

On the other hand, my publisher has yet to review the manuscript after a full year. This is not a slight. My editor is deluged with proposals from unpublished authors that she must read. Can you imagine what it is like to read hundreds of manuscripts a year written by martial arts guys and gun nuts? She knows my stuff is good, so just sets it aside until the economics of publishing dictate a need for something in this category at this length.

I hope by publishing this advance edition that interest in seeing a hardcopy edition will grow and that this will insure or hasten its publication. On the other hand, by putting this out as a humble e-book I might be diminishing its value for later hardcopy publication. There, so I have just rolled the dice in my mind once again. I hope its boxcars.

In closing, I am **James LaFond**, and I approve this edition! Please acquire a Nobel ballot and send in your nomination for *When You're Food* in the non-fiction literature category.

May you enjoy a long serene life.

James LaFond, Friday 13th January 2012

Retrospective

Since I have written that afterward publishing has changed dramatically, to such an extent that I suspect that those small publishing houses such as paladin press who once made it possible for people like me to get published, will have gone the way of the condor by the time I do.

On the other hand I may now publish my own books. Since its publication in 2012 When You're food has been our #1 seller from among our 21 e-book selections at www.jameslafond.com.

Between my agent, Erique Watson, my editor Jamie King, and my cerebrally superior youngest son Glen, who was the five-year-old boy pushing the toy police car around when those thugs came for his older brother and I morphed into a tasteless NRA joke, all 50 of my books that paladin press does not hold the print option on, will be in print, including more titles in this series.

In the years since the publication of When You're Food readers and fighters who I train have asked me to speak to the largely non-physical skill set used in avoiding the lethal levels of violence I have so often skirted by uncomfortably slim margins. The rub is that the margin must be uncomfortably slim in order to avoid the physical expression of this type of predatory violence. It is a double-edged encounter, and must be made uncomfortable. Earlier this year I finally addressed the art of 'autonomous alienation' as I call it in the book Taboo You: Way of the Terminal Man, which is in fact the sequel to When You're Food.

Thanks for taking the time.

Live as free as you can be.

James LaFond, Baltimore Maryland, Monday, 10/27/2014.

The Ala Carte Menu

Here are a few extra tidbits. Dessert if you like after The feast. I tried to put these tales of terror into the context of the principles James and I discussed in terms of predation and human evolutionary characteristics. Also, in my opinion, the good guys win in these encounters. So we end this vale of tears and blood on an uplifting note.

Here is an illustration of the hunting mindset. Did an Indian come out and face the mountain lion or bear in a duel? Of course not!

Vengeance with the Club
A Case of Juvenile Justice

This is an old account from the early 1960s, which occurred in the Belair-Edison neighborhood of Northeast Baltimore. Joey eventually joined the army and became an Army Times reporter in Vietnam, where he earned his purple belt in TaeKwonDo from members of the ROK Tiger Brigade.

Little Joey

#03-35: day, second, first-person aggressor

At age 14 Joey was beginning to get sick of being bullied by the likes of Darby, a 21-year-old who had just shook him down for his pocket change, and was not beyond putting out his cigarette on a boy's chest.

"I picked up this two-by-four and hid behind a shed in the alley. When Darby walked by I took a full swing—I played baseball—and hit him square between the shoulder-blades. There was a good solid thud and he just fell forward and laid there like he was dead. I panicked and ran. I don't think he ever knew who did it."

In general, when clubs are used successfully by a smaller aggressor, stealth or surprise are involved, with a long-standing motivation tending to fuel more effective attacks than do spontaneous altercations.

Here is the example of a low level predator running into the wrong guy and then being feasted upon by opportunists. Darwin gets a plug somewhere in there.

'Picking Parts'
A Lecture from Tattoo Rick on the Transcendent Growth Experienced in Tantric Punk Stomping Sessions

"One Guy was punching him while three other guys were stomping all the loose parts.

.....and three to four guys are stomping his buddy, —they knew what they were doing— ankles, hands, anything that was out."

-Dan

I conducted hundreds of interviews at Tattoo Rick's bar in Northeast Baltimore in the late 1990s. After years of "holding court" behind the bar, Tattoo Rick was a polished speaker and the best interview I ever landed.

#01-23: night, minutes, first-person defender

"I was twenty-five, and had stopped drinking because of my stomach problems. This was back when the city had the gun buy-back thing going. I was working down the GM plant. It was after last call at the bar—a cool fall night. I was with these two guys, on a little street in Fells Point, at the time when there was a lot of vacant houses there. We were headed back to our bikes, which we had parked up from the market. They were walking down the street and I was slightly behind to their right on the narrow sidewalk.

"I sensed somebody behind me and felt something poke me in the back. I instinctively came around with the right elbow and caught him in the temple. He dropped and I heard the clatter of a gun, and I said, 'You mutherfucker! I'm gonna fuckin' kill you!'

"This was back when I was wearing the big biker-engineer boots. So I'm stomping the shit out of this guy. That's when my buds come up and said, 'What are ya doin'?'

"I said, 'This guy tried ta rob me so I'm killin' 'im.'

"They're like, 'Cool dude, and started stompin' him until they got bored, and then kept going. After they stop making noise it kind'a takes the fun out of it. The 'Oh please' phase only lasts ten to fifteen seconds. After that it's just an exercise in futility—just stretching your legs. That's why I always liked those steel-toe boots. A round kick with one of those in your ribs really changes your world.

"I wasn't finished with him—he was still breathing. I played soccer with his head until my legs cramped. The other guys came back, and they're like, 'Come on man, we aren't standing here all night while you stomp this guy.'

"I put a couple of stomps on his head, took the gun, stuck it in my belt, and joined them. When you walk in places like that and aren't prepared ugly things happen to you. When you are prepared, fun things—like this—happen. When we got home my buds said, 'Hey man, let's see the gun.'

"So I pulled it out and checked the clip. It was empty. Then I slid the action back to check the chamber and these fuckin' springs popped out—like boyyyng! And I said, 'Look at this. This fuckin' idiot tried to rob me with a broken gun with no bullets in it! He deserves what he got.'

"The next day I got the gun back together and took it down to the police station. I felt really cool, riding a motorcycle and packing heat! I was hoping the cops would pull me over. I had the gun stuck in my belt in plain view. I walked into the station with this thing hanging out of my belt and said, 'Do you guys want this?'

"They were like, 'Yeah', and asked me where I got it.

"I told them, 'I beat the shit out of some guy in Fells Point and took it from him.'

"They said, 'Yeah, right. So what are you, some kind of karate guy?'

"I said, 'Yeah. As a matter of fact I am.'

"So I told them the whole story and they gave me the fifty bucks. I was hoping the thing wouldn't fall apart in their hands. It was a big forty-five auto.

"I must not have killed the guy, because the police took all the information. I was kind of surprised about that. He was just some skinny white guy, and I left him with his hair matted to his face with blood. Years later two detectives came to my house asking where I got the gun. They said, 'Yeah. That's what it says here.' and left.

"You never forget a good stomping. I love that sound: that 'melon hitting the concrete' sound. When you hear it, its like, 'Ooh yeah, I got a good one!' Its just like when you hit a golf ball just right.

"I don't feel bad about it. I'm a Darwinist. Why is this guy even on my planet? He's breathing my air, taking up my space. Let's thin the herd. Drive the ones like this to the edge so that the predators can eat them. Maybe I fucked this guy up so bad that he couldn't pay his drug debt and his dealer whacked him? Here comes another one that's getting close to the edge of the herd (points to elderly enfeebled alcoholic patron entering the bar with a walker)—good evening sir. What will it be tonight? A fine mass-produced American brew perhaps?"

-Tattoo Rick

This story evokes a hilarious image of these poor chinese people running around screaming while the War of the Gargantuas is occurring in their takeout joint.

Continuing the food connection...

Fish Food
The Mac Daddy and Ma Man in the Hood

I'm in the car, as ma man goin' in ta the Chinese joint, when these otha three dudes is comin' out. I'm five-eleven three-hundred, he five-ten two-fitty. One a them little, two of em big bruthas—six-foot two-fitty. One a them bumps en says, 'What up nigger.' Nasty, like that—E. R.

When You're Food

Ma man say, 'Who you callin' nigger, nigger!' while the two otha dudes commin' up behine. This all happen in the front doorway area of the Chinese joint—the carryout section. They didn't see me, didn't know I was there. He turns sideways and gives me the eye-signal, and I know it's on.

Now, the Mac Daddy normally cool, calm, collective—all 'bout love. We all bruthas—even you—in the eye of the Lord. But when it come time to throw down—ta back up a brutha—The Mac Daddy become a chump-crushin machine! It the fear. You don' wan me ta fear ya; that when the anga come—especially when that word [the N-word] is used nastily. When The Mac Daddy become angray he get the urge ta break ribs en jaws, ta hear the crack a the bones!

Now that not the preferred Mac Daddy persona. I don' wan' the anga en the violence. That why I practice negotiatin.' But den you got some unreasonable dudes...

I walk in like I'm a customer. I knew it was ready time as soon as I heard the conversation. As I headed in I punched this one big dude in the back of the head, right in the side of his ear from behind. He go forward, and ma man is on the otha big dude, crackin' 'im to the floor.

Now this little one standin' in front a me. He was lookin' this way for an escape, look at me, look that way for an escape, look at me—en I punch im in the jaw, twice, jus for bein' there. He go down. No gettin' up for him.

Meanwhile ma man is punishin' this dude for callin' 'im a nigger, stompin' a mudhole in 'is ass—wearin' his ass out. The fist dude comin' to his feet about now, on hands en knees, crawlin' toward this giant fish tank these Chinese people have across the front wall, with these big colaful fish. He was gettin' up, become a threat. So I grabbed im by the back of 'is shirt and shoved 'im. He put out his hand to stop 'iself and it went through the middle of the glass. His head hit the corna of the tank and the whole thing cracked.

The police had been called already—kinda early I thought. You could hear the sirens and all these tiny Chinese people were running around chattering—they couldn't speak much English. The lady though, she was yellin,' 'You get out!'

I said, 'Come on Yo,' to ma man. But he was still stompin' that dude en I had ta pull 'im off. We hauled ass! You don' wanna escape in a car cause someone 'ill get a tag number en the police got ya later on. They hadn't seen us drive up or get out of the car. So we ran to our buddy's house around the corna.

He walked up and got the car. He talked to some people while all the cops and the ambulances was there. The two big dudes was on stretchas. The Chinese people couldn't give a good description, but one customa was tryin'...

You know how some people say some otha people all look the same? So what do the police got? Two big bruthas beatin' down two big bruthas—happens *all the time.*

The final course, literally chowing down on a guy's ear. Hate at second bite.

This PCP Freak
A Legendary Harm City Brawler Recounts His Favorite Fight

Every urban subculture has its most feared actors. In South Baltimore, in the 1980s, it was Duncan, a former Navy jet mechanic who worked as a bouncer, and as a bodyguard for strippers.

An Ear for an Inch

#46-01 to 46-06: night, minutes, first-person

This is from an interview with Duncan. He was highly intelligent, stood six foot four, weighed in at 240, had piercing—almost possessed—eyes, and a thick black beard that grew nearly to his eyes. He could definitely play the heavy in a Rob Zombie film.

"I like violence. Its fun, and is usually over before you're tired. This is my favorite.

I was young—perhaps thirty—and was bouncing at this bar. It's pretty crowded, and this PCP freak—a short stocky guy—starts with this chick and punches her in the jaw. I'm headed across the room. By the time I get there he had punched the girl's boyfriend and the owner.

"I put him in a full-nelson, walked him over to the door, and opened it with his face. Then somebody pushed me out the door. I turned around and this guy's friend was coming out behind me, unhitching his chain belt. I'm between these two, deciding who I'm going to kill first, and my friend—who is a lot bigger than me and just happened to be riding by—stopped his car in the middle of the street and got out. He basically disposed of the twerp with the chain. I don't know what he did because I was busy with the freak.

"As this guy rushes me I punched him in the face (right cross), grabbed him, picked him up, slammed him, and kicked him in the face (with toe of shoe). I also kicked him while he was getting up to charge me again. He kept getting up and charging me. He obviously wasn't feeling a thing. (This sequence was repeated numerous, but uncounted, times.)

I started to get tired, so I got low with a [shoulder] butt, putting it into his chest for a scoop. I feel something and look down and this freak is biting me, trying to tear off a piece. (The resulting sunken scar on Duncan's left shoulder is the size of a silver dollar.)

I'm thinking, 'What the fuck is this?'

Well, two people can play that game, pal. This guy is munching away. I'm going to take something from him too. I look [down] over my shoulder and all I see is this ear. So I bit it and ripped it off. It stayed in my mouth—didn't spit out.

The cops pull up, saw the blood, and took us to the hospital, with the girl he [had] punched. I wasn't hurt but there was blood everywhere. The funniest thing was the ear. It was stuck between my teeth and I couldn't get it out. I wiggled it and worked it and couldn't pull it loose until we got to the hospital. I was treated and released. Of course, the girl was there, and she was real happy with me—real grateful.

[Later] I was charged with maiming and disfiguring. I didn't know there was even a law for that. I just about shit when I found out I was facing twenty years. When I got into court, and saw that the judge was a lady, I thought it was all over.

The guy who lost the ear—a real dirt bag—said his piece. Then it was my turn. I had witnesses, and I told the judge that I had been working as a bouncer, that this guy was hitting patrons and employees. When I ejected him he wanted to fight, and he took the first bite. I said, 'Your Honor, an eye for an eye, a tooth for a tooth. Just like the Bible says, hon.'

She was getting sick. She threw up her hands and said, 'This is disgusting. Everybody just get out of my courtroom.'

She threw it out. I beat the rap and I was sweating it too. Overall I would have to say it was a positive experience; had a great fight, got paid, got laid, beat the charges, and got a souvenir. What's not to like?

I kept it [the ear]. It was about half the ear. A lot more than Tyson got! I put it in a baby food jar, and kept it on the back of the kitchen sink for about a year. Eventually it got really funky so I threw it out.

A couple of years later we met this nice older guy and he said, 'You probably know my son. You're about his age. It was the guy's dad. I said, 'Yeah, probably.'

I didn't have the heart to tell him how well we were acquainted."

That's all folks. Cut your carbs and eat your protein. Stay hungry.

Mescallaneous Thoughts

1. Dress down on your free time. Forget the Alt-right fetish with 'the clothes make the man'. White trash wear always makes you look even slightly dangerous. Urban armor. Lots of pockets with hands in them generate the unknown quality that serves as a first defense screen. A platform from which to work from and utilize options. Learn to love camo pants and hoodies. Who needs a girlfriend?
2. Get in the habit of walking closer to males who flex on you to get you conditioned to the mindset of closing and to overturn their preconceived selection process for aggression.
3. Lift weights and be as strong and fit as you can. It can't hurt as long as you know that it

is not the be all, end all. You gotta box, grapple or stickfight, even just a little.

4. You will get the battery acid adrenaline taste in your mouth unless you are used to contact through boxing or another combat sport. Understand that's what it is and not fear.

5. Don't say a word or talk to anyone. Just look through, around and walk off.

6. Acting crazy has a place sometimes, especially repeating what is said to you over and over. Crazy people seem to operate on a loop like a repeating malfunctioning CD player. When the cops show up you become joe normal. You do not want to break the law. Be weird crazy not aggressive crazy. Like a fox.

7. Develop a code of honor and meditate on it daily. Do NOT extend it to the dishonorable. Don't be a sap or a simp.

8. Don't agonize over a mistake. Learn from it. Easy to say and the hardest thing to do.

9. Finally drop the ideals that have any link to the way things 'ought to be' or 'I have the right' or anything linked to the historic American nation. Whether it ever was something good at one point or not; it is not now. Survive physically, mentally and legally. There is beer to drink, books to read and maybe even a woman who is not totally disgusted by you out there who you might come across.

10. This crap always shows up when you are not ready, preoccupied or not expecting it. There is a god and his name is Murphy.